# The 5 Elements of Effective Learning

# Contents

## Introduction

This book is designed to be used as a practical resource for your classroom. Each page has a visual example which can be converted into a classroom resource. The resources can be used as:

(i)     laminated cards in learning-to-learn lessons
(ii)    converted to PowerPoint slides for your whiteboard
(iii)   enlarged for classroom displays around the school
(iv)    printed as worksheets for learning-to-learn lessons
(v)     photocopied into learning-to-learn booklets for tutors, parents

If you find the book useful, you can get a taster of my whiteboard resources at www.kija.co.uk.

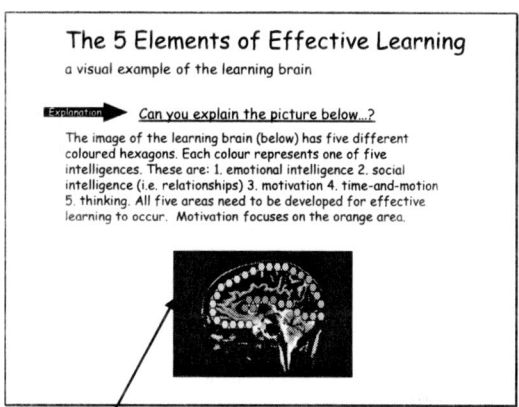

'The 5 Elements of Effective Learning' explains my learning theory in a nutshell.

As you'll see in the image above, there is a chain of hexagons going around in the edge of the brain.

The chain represents five distinct areas. All five areas link to create a 'domino' effect of learning.

The five areas are:

1. Emotional intelligence
2. Relationship skills
3. Motivation
4. Time-and-motion
5. Thinking skills

All five areas need to be developed for successful learning to occur.

This book explains each of the five elements and provides you with simple strategies to develop each element in your classroom.

When used regularly, 'The 5 Elements of Effective Learning' transforms students' achievement.

Element 1 – Emotional Intelligence

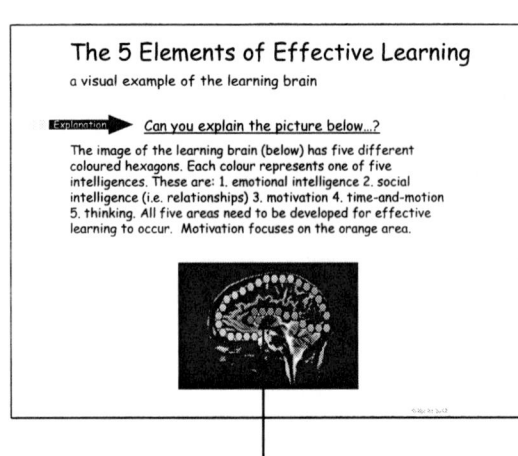

'Emotional Intelligence' is the first of the five elements. In the image above, emotional intelligence is represented by the six hexagons beginning the chain. There are six hexagons because each area has six skills. The six skills for 'Emotional Intelligence' are:

1.Empathy    2.Dignity    3.Humility    4.Relativity    5.Sensitivity    6.Sympathy

Why is 'Emotional Intelligence' element one...?

Because teachers and students need to understand and manage their emotions to create a positive learning environment where learning can flourish. 'Emotional Intelligence' is the ability to understand and manage our feelings. This is why it's the first element.

The first section of the book is, therefore, on the six emotional intelligence skills.

You will see an image above each page, providing with a resource to go along with the skill.

## Empathy

understand

Empathy is the ability to understand how someone else feels about a situation. This is a *very powerful* relationship-skill because it helps you to work out peoples' moods and reactions to things.

Empathy is the ability to *take yourself out of the equation* when you're trying to understand someone else's behaviour/mood. By putting your feelings to one side, you allow the other person's feelings 'in'. At this point, you begin to understand their feelings/needs better.

The explanation image (above) on 'Empathy' is designed for 'big picture' learners.

'Big picture' learners are concrete thinkers who need to able to visualise an idea in a practical situation.

The explanation for 'Empathy' (above) paints a picture of what empathy 'looks like' in the classroom.

How do I use it...? Convert the image (above) to your own PowerPoint slide and display it on your whiteboard. Alternatively, enlarge the image, laminate it and display it in your room, ready for use.

When do I use it...? Think about using the explanation image as your starter to help students make the connection between empathy, behaviour, listening and learning.

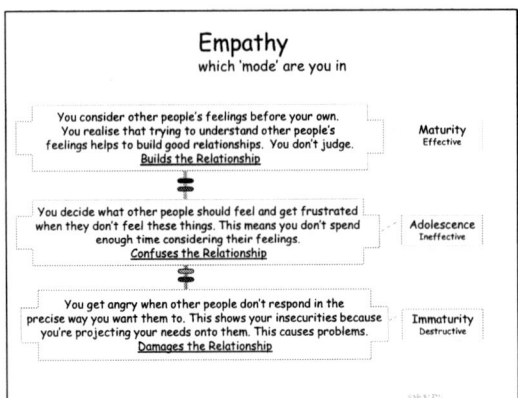

The '3 modes' image (above) is like holding up a mirror for your students and helping them to reflect on their current level of empathy.

The small coloured boxes on the right-hand side highlight whether a student is in active, active-passive or passive mode. The use of these three modes helps students to see the impact of their level of empathy on their behaviour and attitude in lessons.

How do I use it...? Convert the image (above) to your own PowerPoint slide and display it on your whiteboard. Alternatively, enlarge the image, laminate it and display it in your room, ready for use.

When do I use it...? Use the '3 modes' image during your lesson to re-establish students' need to have empathy to 'listen and learn' in lessons.

Empathy 'Tips'
understand

When you're frustrated or angry with someone, *put your needs and feelings down* and stand where they're standing. Why...? Because empathy is the ability to *look down on a situation* and 'see' and 'feel' what the other person is feeling.

If you fall out with someone, look at *yourself first*. Why...? Because looking at yourself is what the other person is doing—they're looking and responding to *you*. See' what they see to feel their anger/hurt.

The 'Empathy Tips' image (above) is a visual example of how to develop students' empathy.

This provides with concrete strategies they can start using in school and life.

How do I use it...? Convert the image (above) to your own PowerPoint slide and display it on your whiteboard. Alternatively, enlarge the image, laminate it and display it in your room, ready for use.

When do I use it...? Keep referring the 'Empathy' and phrases such as "put your needs down" to create the link between empathy, behaviour, listening and learning.

Empathy
plenary: reflection

Use the 'prompts' to talk about your mature state of empathy

"Even if I didn't immediately see their point, I valued it so that..."
"I tried to focus on what everyone else needed first which..."

Builds the Relationship

Maturity
Effective

Use the 'prompts' to talk about your adolescent state of empathy

"I listened to other people but didn't really value their ideas so..."
"I got frustrated when people didn't see things my way which..."

Confuses the Relationship

Adolescence
Ineffective

Use the 'prompts' to talk about your immature state of empathy

"I couldn't really see where other people were coming from which..."
"I couldn't really see beyond my own needs and I think this..."

Damages the Relationship

Immaturity
Destructive

The 'Empathy' plenary image (above) is a powerful way of students evaluating their current level of empathy.

The plenary image also helps students to build a 'language of empathy'.

If you look at the image (above), you'll notice that the sentences inside the boxes are incomplete.

The idea is that students decide where they are then complete the sentence to articulate their current level of empathy.

The benefit of the plenary slide is that students need to communicate their understanding and, therefore, are beginning to become more aware of the importance of empathy to behaviour, listening and learning.

When do I use it...?  Use the 'Empathy: plenary' image in your lesson-plenary to review the skill.

Dignity

respect

Dignity is respecting others (and yourself) at all times.

Dignity is a particularly important skill in a world full of pressures and competitiveness.

Dignity is having the emotional intelligence to understand that *kindness is always more important than 'bitching' and competitiveness.*

The explanation image (above) on 'Dignity' is designed for 'big picture' learners.

'Big picture' learners are concrete thinkers who need to able to visualise an idea in a practical situation.

The explanation for 'Dignity' (above) paints a picture of what dignity 'looks like' in the classroom.

How do I use it...? Convert the image (above) to your own PowerPoint slide and display it on your whiteboard. Alternatively, enlarge the image, laminate it and display it in your room, ready for use.

When do I use it...? Think about using the explanation image as your starter to help students make the connection between dignity, behaviour and learning.

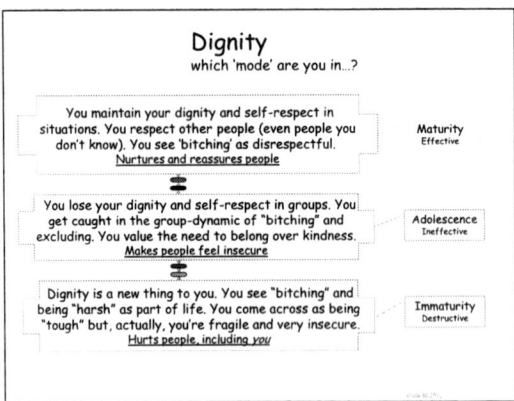

The '3 modes' image (above) is like holding up a mirror for your students and helping them to reflect on their current level of dignity.

The small coloured boxes on the right-hand side highlight whether a student is in active, active-passive or passive mode. The use of these three modes helps students to see the impact of their level of dignity on their behaviour and attitude in lessons.

How do I use it...? Convert the image (above) to your own PowerPoint slide and display it on your whiteboard. Alternatively, enlarge the image, laminate it and display it in your room, ready for use.

When do I use it...? Use the '3 modes' image during your lesson to re-establish students' need to have dignity to 'be respectful, behave and learn' in lessons.

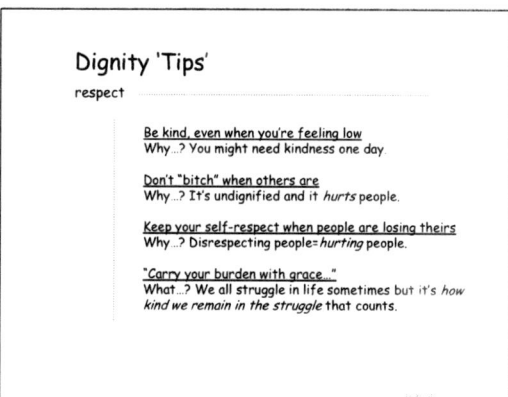

The 'Dignity Tips' image (above) is a visual example of how to develop students' dignity.

This provides with concrete strategies they can start using in school and life.

How do I use it...? Convert the image (above) to your own PowerPoint slide and display it on your whiteboard. Alternatively, enlarge the image, laminate it and display it in your room, ready for use.

When do I use it...? Keep referring the 'Dignity' and phrases such as "don't lose your dignity" to create the link between dignity, manners and behaviour.

The 'Dignity' plenary image (above) is a powerful way of students evaluating their current level of dignity.

The plenary image also helps students to build a 'language of dignity'.

If you look at the image (above), you'll notice that the sentences inside the boxes are incomplete.

The idea is that students decide where they are then complete the sentence to articulate their current level of dignity.

The benefit of the plenary slide is that students need to communicate their understanding and, therefore, are beginning to become more aware of the importance of dignity to behaviour and learning.

When do I use it...? Use the 'Dignity: plenary' image in your lesson-plenary to review the skill.

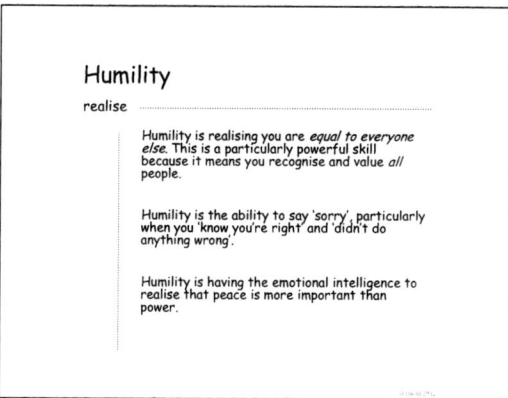

The explanation image (above) on 'Humility' is designed for 'big picture' learners.

'Big picture' learners are concrete thinkers who need to able to visualise an idea in a practical situation.

The explanation for 'Humility' (above) paints a picture of what humility 'looks like' in the classroom.

How do I use it...? Convert the image (above) to your own PowerPoint slide and display it on your whiteboard. Alternatively, enlarge the image, laminate it and display it in your room, ready for use.

When do I use it...? Think about using the explanation image as your starter to help students make the connection between humility, manners, behaviour and learning.

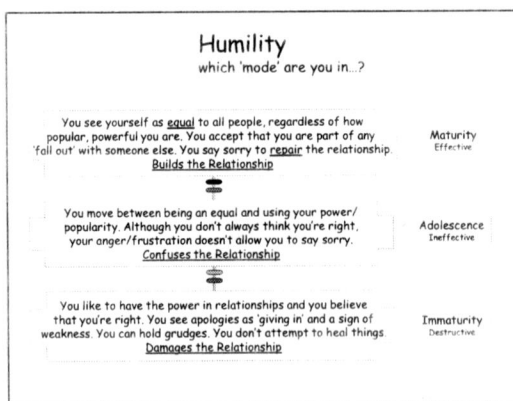

The '3 modes' image (above) is like holding up a mirror for your students and helping them to reflect on their current level of humility.

The small coloured boxes on the right-hand side highlight whether a student is in active, active-passive or passive mode. The use of these three modes helps students to see the impact of their level of humility on their behaviour and attitude in lessons.

How do I use it...? Convert the image (above) to your own PowerPoint slide and display it on your whiteboard. Alternatively, enlarge the image, laminate it and display it in your room, ready for use.

When do I use it...? Use the '3 modes' image during your lesson to re-establish students' need to have humility to 'be respectful, behave and learn' in lessons.

**Humility 'Tips'**

realise

If you've annoyed someone, apologise
<u>Why...?</u> This reinforces you value them
and removes any shared anxiety=*peace*.

If you're the one with the power, give
others a feeling of power.
<u>Why...?</u> Because power is only good if it's
used to *build others*.

*'All rivers and streams meet at
the ocean—at the same level.'*

The 'Humility Tips' image (above) is a visual example of how to develop students' humility.

This provides with concrete strategies they can start using in school and life.

<u>How do I use it...?</u>  Convert the image (above) to your own PowerPoint slide and display it on your whiteboard. Alternatively, enlarge the image, laminate it and display it in your room, ready for use.

<u>When do I use it...?</u> Keep referring the 'Humility' to create the link between humility, manners and behaviour.

Humility
plenary: reflection

Use the 'prompts' to talk about your mature state of humility

" Even if I'm good at something, I know it doesn't make me better than..."
" I'll always say sorry if I fall out with someone. I know this helps to..."

Maturity
Effective

Builds the Relationship

Use the 'prompts' to talk about your adolescent state of humility

" I sometimes confuse being good at something with being 'better' but..."
" I'll only say sorry if I think something is my fault. I need to learn to..."

Adolescence
Ineffective

Confuses the Relationship

Use the 'prompts' to talk about your immature state of humility

" I lose my self-respect and respect for others when I'm angry which..."
" I almost never say sorry because I see it as 'giving in'. I can see now ..."

Immaturity
Destructive

Damages the Relationship

The 'Humility' plenary image (above) is a powerful way of students evaluating their current level of humility.

The plenary image also helps students to build a 'language of humility'.

If you look at the image (above), you'll notice that the sentences inside the boxes are incomplete.

The idea is that students decide where they are then complete the sentence to articulate their current level of humility.

The benefit of the plenary slide is that students need to communicate their understanding and, therefore, are beginning to become more aware of the importance of humility to behaviour and learning.

When do I use it...? Use the 'Humility: plenary' image in your lesson-plenary to review the skill.

**Relativity**

embrace

Relativity is the ability to accept and embrace *difference* in life rather than judge or fear it.

Relativity is having the emotional intelligence to understand that there *are lots of ways of living, doing, dressing, feeling, thinking* and these are all of *equal value.*

*"It doesn't matter how you travel, as long as you arrive."*

The explanation image (above) on 'Relativity' is designed for 'big picture' learners.

'Big picture' learners are concrete thinkers who need to able to visualise an idea in a practical situation.

The explanation for 'Relativity' (above) paints a picture of what relativity 'looks like' in the classroom.

How do I use it...? Convert the image (above) to your own PowerPoint slide and display it on your whiteboard. Alternatively, enlarge the image, laminate it and display it in your room, ready for use.

When do I use it...? Think about using the explanation image as your starter to help students make the connection between relativity, open-mindedness and acceptance of others in lessons.

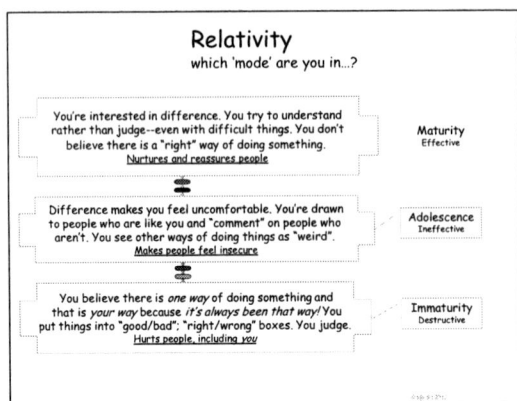

The '3 modes' image (above) is like holding up a mirror for your students and helping them to reflect on their current level of relativity.

The small coloured boxes on the right-hand side highlight whether a student is in active, active-passive or passive mode. The use of these three modes helps students to see the impact of their level of relativity on their behaviour and attitude in lessons.

How do I use it...? Convert the image (above) to your own PowerPoint slide and display it on your whiteboard. Alternatively, enlarge the image, laminate it and display it in your room, ready for use.

When do I use it...? Use the '3 modes' image during your lesson to re-establish students' need to have relativity to 'be respectful of others' choices and opinions' in order to actively engage and listen in lessons.

**Relativity 'tips'**

embrace

1. try to <u>understand</u> rather than judge by considering *the other person's* way-of-life

2. try to see difference as *interesting* rather than *weird*

3. try to see the <u>value</u> in *all things and people* and realise that other ways are just *alternative ways* that aren't *your way.* No better, no worse.

The 'Relativity Tips' image (above) is a visual example of how to develop students' relativity.

This provides with concrete strategies they can start using in school and life.

<u>How do I use it...?</u> Convert the image (above) to your own PowerPoint slide and display it on your whiteboard. Alternatively, enlarge the image, laminate it and display it in your room, ready for use.

<u>When do I use it...?</u> Keep referring the 'Relativity' to create the link between relativity, open-mindedness, respect and behaviour.

The 'Relativity' plenary image (above) is a powerful way of students evaluating their current level of relativity.

The plenary image also helps students to build a 'language of relativity'.

If you look at the image (above), you'll notice that the sentences inside the boxes are incomplete.

The idea is that students decide where they are then complete the sentence to articulate their current level of relativity.

The benefit of the plenary slide is that students need to communicate their understanding and, therefore, are beginning to become more aware of the importance of relativity to behaviour and learning.

When do I use it...? Use the 'Relativity: plenary' image in your lesson-plenary to review the skill.

## Sympathy

care

Sympathy is the ability to show kindness when other people are suffering.

Sympathy is the ability to care and support people at their most fragile.

Sympathy is having the emotional intelligence to understand that *caring* is more important than judging.

The explanation image (above) on 'Sympathy' is designed for 'big picture' learners.

'Big picture' learners are concrete thinkers who need to able to visualise an idea in a practical situation.

The explanation for 'Sympathy' (above) paints a picture of what sympathy 'looks like' in the classroom.

How do I use it...? Convert the image (above) to your own PowerPoint slide and display it on your whiteboard. Alternatively, enlarge the image, laminate it and display it in your room, ready for use.

When do I use it...? Think about using the explanation image as your starter to help students make the connection between sympathy and 'mood awareness': i.e. responding and helping when others are struggling.

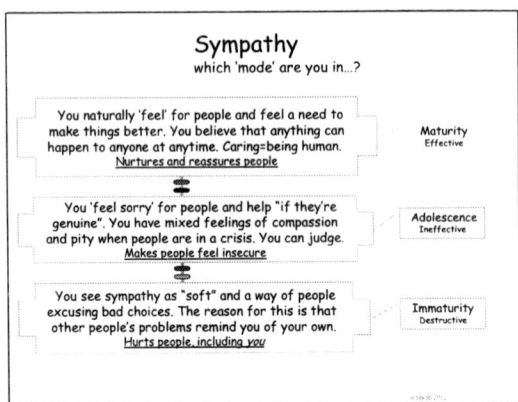

The '3 modes' image (above) is like holding up a mirror for your students and helping them to reflect on their current level of sympathy.

The small coloured boxes on the right-hand side highlight whether a student is in active, active-passive or passive mode. The use of these three modes helps students to see the impact of their level of sympathy on their behaviour and attitude in lessons.

How do I use it...? Convert the image (above) to your own PowerPoint slide and display it on your whiteboard. Alternatively, enlarge the image, laminate it and display it in your room, ready for use.

When do I use it...? Use the '3 modes' image during your lesson to re-establish students' need to have sympathy to 'know when others need help and understanding'.

**Sympathy 'Tips'**

care

① Try to care and support without judgement when people around you are struggling.

Why...? Because *being there* and *helping* are often more important than words in a crisis.

② When you feel someone's pain, try to do something simple to take it away.

Like what...? Smiling; a tap on the shoulder; praise Why...? So people feel less alone.

The 'Sympathy Tips' image (above) is a visual example of how to develop students' sympathy.

This provides with concrete strategies they can start using in school and life.

How do I use it...? Convert the image (above) to your own PowerPoint slide and display it on your whiteboard. Alternatively, enlarge the image, laminate it and display it in your room, ready for use.

When do I use it...? Keep referring the 'Sympathy' to create the link between sympathy and 'mood awareness': i.e. recognising and helping others in need.

The 'Sympathy' plenary image (above) is a powerful way of students evaluating their current level of sympathy.

The plenary image also helps students to build a 'language of sympathy'.

If you look at the image (above), you'll notice that the sentences inside the boxes are incomplete.

The idea is that students decide where they are then complete the sentence to articulate their current level of sympathy.

The benefit of the plenary slide is that students need to communicate their understanding and, therefore, are beginning to become more aware of the importance of sympathy to behaviour and learning.

When do I use it...? Use the 'Sympathy: plenary' image in your lesson-plenary to review the skill.

Sensitivity

recognise

Sensitivity is the ability to read other people's moods/feelings.

Sensitivity is being able to adapt what you say based on the other person's moods/feelings.

Sensitivity is having the emotional intelligence to 'pick up on' another person's needs. E.g. You 'pick up' that a friend feels undervalued so you *praise them* to show them that they're valued.

The explanation image (above) on 'Sensitivity' is designed for 'big picture' learners.

'Big picture' learners are concrete thinkers who need to able to visualise an idea in a practical situation.

The explanation for 'Sensitivity' (above) paints a picture of what sensitivity 'looks like' in the classroom.

How do I use it...? Convert the image (above) to your own PowerPoint slide and display it on your whiteboard. Alternatively, enlarge the image, laminate it and display it in your room, ready for use.

When do I use it...? Think about using the explanation image as your starter to help students make the connection between sensitivity and 'consideration of needs': i.e. adapting your needs to the needs of others/the group.

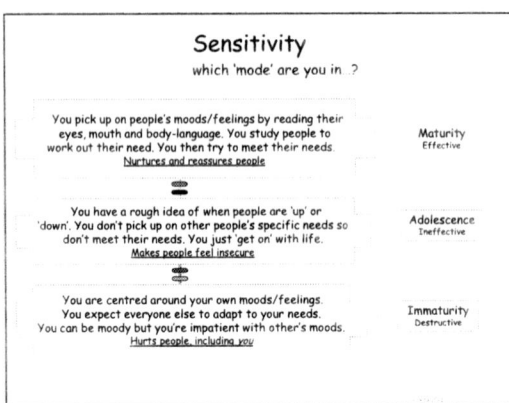

The '3 modes' image (above) is like holding up a mirror for your students and helping them to reflect on their current level of sensitivity.

The small coloured boxes on the right-hand side highlight whether a student is in active, active-passive or passive mode. The use of these three modes helps students to see the impact of their level of sensitivity on their behaviour and attitude in lessons.

How do I use it...? Convert the image (above) to your own PowerPoint slide and display it on your whiteboard. Alternatively, enlarge the image, laminate it and display it in your room, ready for use.

When do I use it...? Use the '3 modes' image during your lesson to re-establish students' need to have sensitivity to 'adapt your mood to the mood of the group' to sustain an effective climate for learning.

## Sensitivity 'Tips'

recognise

(1) Watch/study people before you speak or act. Why...? Because studying someone helps you to work-out the responses they need from you.

(2) Study people's eyes (red/glazed over=low). And..? Say hello and smile if people look low (whoever they are).

(3) Watch people's posture. Why...? The more stooped they are, the weaker they feel. So...? Praise them. Praise=power!

The 'Sensitivity Tips' image (above) is a visual example of how to develop students' sensitivity.

This provides with concrete strategies they can start using in school and life.

How do I use it...? Convert the image (above) to your own PowerPoint slide and display it on your whiteboard. Alternatively, enlarge the image, laminate it and display it in your room, ready for use.

When do I use it...? Keep referring the 'sensitivity' to create the link between sensitivity and 'mood awareness': i.e. adapting to the mood of the group to sustain an effective climate for learning.

The 'Sensitivity' plenary image (above) is a powerful way of students evaluating their current level of sensitivity.

The plenary image also helps students to build a 'language of sensitivity'.

If you look at the image (above), you'll notice that the sentences inside the boxes are incomplete.

The idea is that students decide where they are then complete the sentence to articulate their current level of sensitivity.

The benefit of the plenary slide is that students need to communicate their understanding and, therefore, are beginning to become more aware of the importance of sensitivity to behaviour and learning.

<u>When do I use it...?</u> Use the 'Sensitivity: plenary' image in your lesson-plenary to review the skill.

Element 2 – Relationship Skills

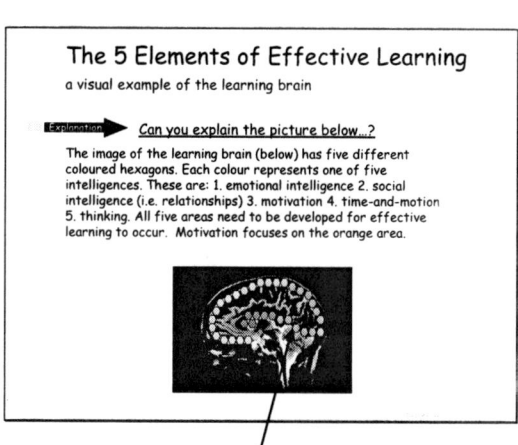

'Relationship Skills' is the second of the five elements. In the image above, relationship-skills is represented by the second chain of hexagons. There are six hexagons because each area has six skills. The six skills for 'Relationships' are:

1.Gesture    2.Humour    3.Tone    4.Listening    5.Engaging    6.Praise

Why is 'Relationship Skills' element two...?

Because once teachers and students are able to understand and manage their own feelings (i.e. emotional intelligence – element one), they are able to build positive relationships. Developing positive relationships builds a student's confidence, making them feel secure enough to take risks – a key aspect of learning. This is why 'relationship skills' is the second element.

The second section of the book is, therefore, on the six relationship skills.

You will see an image above each page, providing with a resource to go along with the skill.

The explanation image (above) on 'Gesture' is designed for 'big picture' learners.

'Big picture' learners are concrete thinkers who need to able to visualise an idea in a practical situation.

The explanation for 'Gesture' (above) paints a picture of what gesture 'looks like' in the classroom.

How do I use it...? Convert the image (above) to your own PowerPoint slide and display it on your whiteboard. Alternatively, enlarge the image, laminate it and display it in your room, ready for use.

When do I use it...? Think about using the explanation image as your starter to help students make the connection between gesture and 'relationship-building' in lessons.

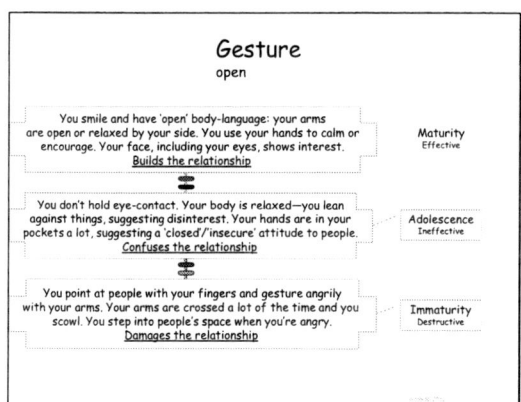

The '3 modes' image (above) is like holding up a mirror for your students and helping them to reflect on their current level of gesture.

The small coloured boxes on the right-hand side highlight whether a student is in active, active-passive or passive mode. The use of these three modes helps students to see the impact of their level of gesture on their behaviour and attitude in lessons.

How do I use it...? Convert the image (above) to your own PowerPoint slide and display it on your whiteboard. Alternatively, enlarge the image, laminate it and display it in your room, ready for use.

When do I use it...? Use the '3 modes' image during your lesson to re-establish students' need to have good gesture to 'build positive relationships' in lessons so that you feel happy and motivated to learn.

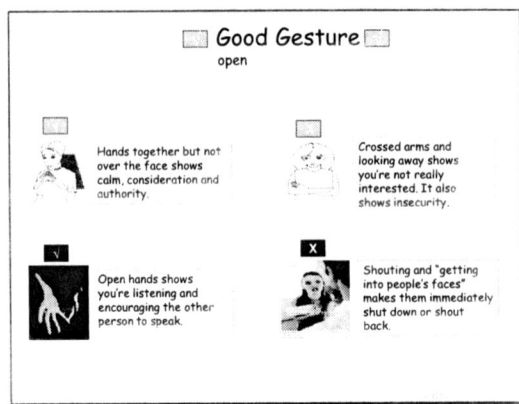

The 'Good Gesture' image (above) is a visual example of how to develop students' awareness of what good gesture looks like.

This provides with concrete strategies they can start using in school and life.

How do I use it...? Convert the image (above) to your own PowerPoint slide and display it on your whiteboard. Alternatively, enlarge the image, laminate it and display it in your room, ready for use.

When do I use it...? Keep referring the 'gesture' to create the link between good gesture and 'good relationships' to connect and motivate you in your lessons.

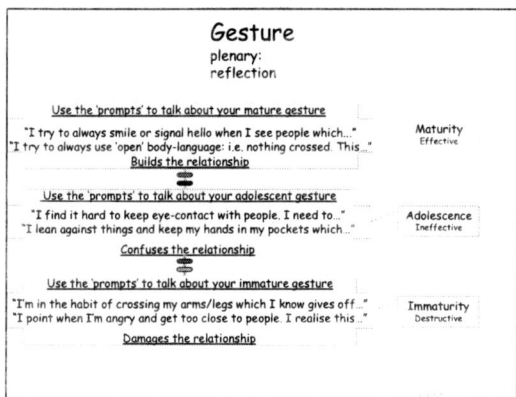

The 'Gesture' plenary image (above) is a powerful way of students evaluating their current level of gesture.

The plenary image also helps students to build a 'language of gesture'.

If you look at the image (above), you'll notice that the sentences inside the boxes are incomplete.

The idea is that students decide where they are then complete the sentence to articulate their current level of gesture.

The benefit of the plenary slide is that students need to communicate their understanding and, therefore, are beginning to become more aware of the importance of gesture to 'relationship-building' and learning.

When do I use it...? Use the 'Gesture: plenary' image in your lesson-plenary to review the skill.

> **Humour**
> smile
>
> Humour is one of the key elements in relationships—the ability to laugh at the world and yourself. Humour improves your mood and the mood of others.
>
> Humour has a 'levelling' influence in relationships, quickly putting people at ease and establishing a positive, safe environment where each person is equally valued.

The explanation image (above) on 'Humour' is designed for 'big picture' learners.

'Big picture' learners are concrete thinkers who need to able to visualise an idea in a practical situation.

The explanation for 'Gesture' (above) paints a picture of what humour 'looks like' in the classroom.

<u>How do I use it...?</u> Convert the image (above) to your own PowerPoint slide and display it on your whiteboard. Alternatively, enlarge the image, laminate it and display it in your room, ready for use.

<u>When do I use it...?</u> Think about using the explanation image as your starter to help students make the connection between humour and 'relationship-building' in lessons.

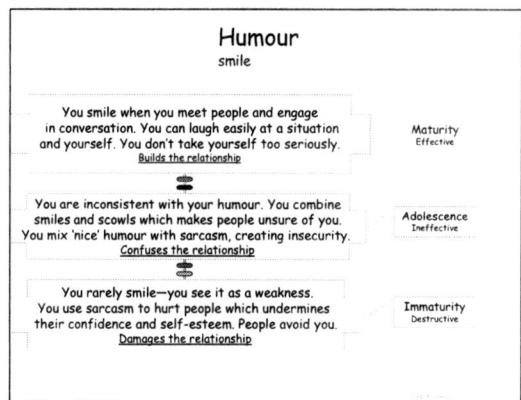

The '3 modes' image (above) is like holding up a mirror for your students and helping them to reflect on their current level of humour.

The small coloured boxes on the right-hand side highlight whether a student is in active, active-passive or passive mode. The use of these three modes helps students to see the impact of their level of humour on their behaviour and attitude in lessons.

How do I use it...? Convert the image (above) to your own PowerPoint slide and display it on your whiteboard. Alternatively, enlarge the image, laminate it and display it in your room, ready for use.

When do I use it...? Use the '3 modes' image during your lesson to re-establish students' need to have good humour to 'build positive relationships' in lessons so that you feel happy and motivated to learn.

**Humour**

tips

- Smile as you arrive in the morning
- Smile, keeping eye-contact, as you walk past people
- See the funny side of things—it helps you to deal with life much better and reduces stress
- When you smile, or make someone else smile, you charm them and make them happy

The 'Humour Tips' image (above) is a visual example of how to develop students' awareness of how to use humour effectively to build positive relationships.

This provides with concrete strategies they can start using in school and life.

How do I use it...? Convert the image (above) to your own PowerPoint slide and display it on your whiteboard. Alternatively, enlarge the image, laminate it and display it in your room, ready for use.

When do I use it...? Keep referring the 'humour' to create the link between good humour and 'good relationships' to connect and motivate you in your lessons.

Humour
plenary: reflection

Use the 'prompts' to talk about your mature humour
"I try not take myself too seriously. I can laugh at myself which..."
"I use humour to defuse 'heated' situations. This helps to..."
Builds the relationship

Maturity
Effective

Use the 'prompts' to talk about your adolescent humour
"I use humour to 'put people in their place'. I need to start..."
"I wear my mood on my face'. I think I need to maintain a positive..."
Confuses the relationship

Adolescence
Ineffective

Use the 'prompts' to talk about your immature humour
"I don't smile for the sake of it. I saw it as false before but..."
"I can be sarcastic which, I realise now, hurts people. I need to..."
Damages the relationship

Immaturity
Destructive

The 'Humour' plenary image (above) is a powerful way of students evaluating their current level of humour.

The plenary image also helps students to build a 'language of humour'.

If you look at the image (above), you'll notice that the sentences inside the boxes are incomplete.

The idea is that students decide where they are then complete the sentence to articulate their current level of humour.

The benefit of the plenary slide is that students need to communicate their understanding and, therefore, are beginning to become more aware of the importance of humour to 'relationship-building' and learning.

When do I use it...? Use the 'Humour: plenary' image in your lesson-plenary to review the skill.

**Tone**
*calm*

Your tone-of-voice tells other people a lot about you.

Your tone-of-voice can also affect other people, making them feel happy, safe, insecure, patronised etc.

Your tone-of-voice has an impact on a person's mood and self-esteem.

The explanation image (above) on 'Tone' is designed for 'big picture' learners.

'Big picture' learners are concrete thinkers who need to able to visualise an idea in a practical situation.

The explanation for 'Tone' (above) paints a picture of what tone 'looks like' in the classroom.

How do I use it...? Convert the image (above) to your own PowerPoint slide and display it on your whiteboard. Alternatively, enlarge the image, laminate it and display it in your room, ready for use.

When do I use it...? Think about using the explanation image as your starter to help students make the connection between tone and 'relationship-building' in lessons.

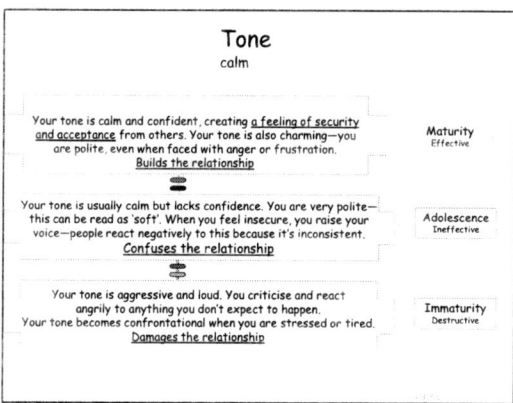

The '3 modes' image (above) is like holding up a mirror for your students and helping them to reflect on their current level of tone.

The small coloured boxes on the right-hand side highlight whether a student is in active, active-passive or passive mode. The use of these three modes helps students to see the impact of their level of tone on their behaviour and attitude in lessons.

How do I use it...? Convert the image (above) to your own PowerPoint slide and display it on your whiteboard. Alternatively, enlarge the image, laminate it and display it in your room, ready for use.

When do I use it...? Use the '3 modes' image during your lesson to re-establish students' need to have good tone to 'build positive relationships' in lessons so that you feel happy and motivated to learn.

Tone 'tips'
calm

Keep your voice calm when faced with
angry/annoyed people=will reduce conflict.

Use a reassuring, calm tone. This helps
people feel valued and secure.

Use a soothing tone in sensitive situations
("You okay?"), "Can I get you anything...?").
This eases the person's anxiety, pain, isolation.

The 'Tone Tips' image (above) is a visual example of how to develop students' awareness of how to use tone effectively to build positive relationships.

This provides with concrete strategies they can start using in school and life.

How do I use it...? Convert the image (above) to your own PowerPoint slide and display it on your whiteboard. Alternatively, enlarge the image, laminate it and display it in your room, ready for use.

When do I use it...? Keep referring the 'tone' to create the link between good tone and 'good relationships' to connect and motivate you in your lessons.

The 'Tone' plenary image (above) is a powerful way of students evaluating their current level of tone.

The plenary image also helps students to build a 'language of tone'.

If you look at the image (above), you'll notice that the sentences inside the boxes are incomplete.

The idea is that students decide where they are then complete the sentence to articulate their current level of tone.

The benefit of the plenary slide is that students need to communicate their understanding and, therefore, are beginning to become more aware of the importance of tone to 'relationship-building' and learning.

When do I use it...?  Use the 'Tone: plenary' image in your lesson-plenary to review the skill.

**Listening**

connect

The skill of listening is one of the hardest skills to learn.

This is because students often think that listening means "not talking".

Good listening is based on your ability to *put your needs down* and focus on someone else. Listening shows that you *care* about other people which improves their mood.

The explanation image (above) on 'Listening' is designed for 'big picture' learners.

'Big picture' learners are concrete thinkers who need to able to visualise an idea in a practical situation.

The explanation for 'Listening' (above) paints a picture of what listening 'looks like' in the classroom.

How do I use it...? Convert the image (above) to your own PowerPoint slide and display it on your whiteboard. Alternatively, enlarge the image, laminate it and display it in your room, ready for use.

When do I use it...? Think about using the explanation image as your starter to help students make the connection between listening and 'active learning' in lessons.

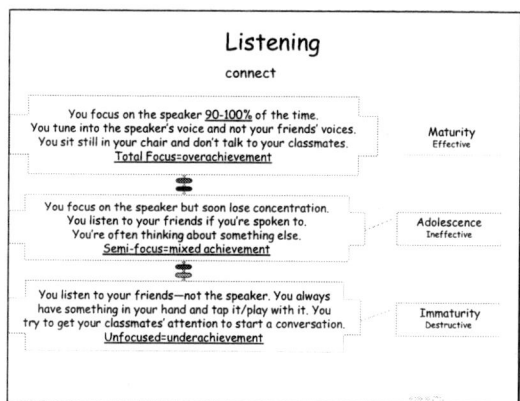

The '3 modes' image (above) is like holding up a mirror for your students and helping them to reflect on their current level of listening.

The small coloured boxes on the right-hand side highlight whether a student is in active, active-passive or passive mode. The use of these three modes helps students to see the impact of their level of listening on their active learning and behaviour in lessons.

How do I use it...? Convert the image (above) to your own PowerPoint slide and display it on your whiteboard. Alternatively, enlarge the image, laminate it and display it in your room, ready for use.

When do I use it...? Use the '3 modes' image during your lesson to re-establish students' need to have good listening to 'active learning' in lessons.

> ## Listening
> the 5 steps
>
> 1. Focus on the speaker (look at them)
> 2. Listen carefully to them (tune in to their voice)
> 3. Register ("log") what they're saying in your head
> 4. Process (turn over) what they've said in your head
> 5. Respond to what's been said (do something with it)

The '5 Steps of Listening' image (above) is a visual example of how to develop students' awareness of how to listen effectively in order to learn actively (and engage fully) in lessons.

This provides with concrete strategies they can start using in school and life.

How do I use it...? Convert the image (above) to your own PowerPoint slide and display it on your whiteboard. Alternatively, enlarge the image, laminate it and display it in your room, ready for use.

When do I use it...? Keep referring the 'listen' to create the link between good listening and 'active learning' in lessons.

The 'Listening' plenary image (above) is a powerful way of students evaluating their current level of listening.

The plenary image also helps students to build a 'language of listening'.

If you look at the image (above), you'll notice that the sentences inside the boxes are incomplete.

The idea is that students decide where they are then complete the sentence to articulate their current level of listening.

The benefit of the plenary slide is that students need to communicate their understanding and, therefore, are beginning to become more aware of the importance of listening to 'active learning'.

When do I use it...? Use the 'Listening: plenary' image in your lesson-plenary to review the skill.

> ## Engaging
> include
>
> The relationship skill of engaging is about including other people.
>
> Including other people is a particularly important skill when you're in a group.
>
> Group-dynamics mean someone is always left-out. Engaging is the skill of recognising when someone is being left out and *including* them, making them feel valued.

The explanation image (above) on 'Engaging' is designed for 'big picture' learners.

'Big picture' learners are concrete thinkers who need to able to visualise an idea in a practical situation.

The explanation for 'Engaging' (above) paints a picture of what engaging 'looks like' in the classroom.

How do I use it...? Convert the image (above) to your own PowerPoint slide and display it on your whiteboard. Alternatively, enlarge the image, laminate it and display it in your room, ready for use.

When do I use it...? Think about using the explanation image as your starter to help students make the connection between engaging and 'active learning' in lessons.

The '3 modes' image (above) is like holding up a mirror for your students and helping them to reflect on their current level of engaging.

The small coloured boxes on the right-hand side highlight whether a student is in active, active-passive or passive mode. The use of these three modes helps students to see the impact of their level of engagement on their active learning and behaviour in lessons.

How do I use it...? Convert the image (above) to your own PowerPoint slide and display it on your whiteboard. Alternatively, enlarge the image, laminate it and display it in your room, ready for use.

When do I use it...? Use the '3 modes' image during your lesson to re-establish students' need to be "actively engaged to actively learn" in lessons.

Engaging
the 5 steps

1. When you're in a group, study everyone

2. Don't dominate in group situations

3. Focus on the quiet person/people in the group

4. Make a compliment to the quiet person/people

5. Ask the opinion of the quiet person/people

The '5 Steps of Engaging' image (above) is a visual example of how to develop students' awareness of how to engage effectively in order to learn actively in lessons.

This provides with concrete strategies they can start using in school and life.

<u>How do I use it...?</u> Convert the image (above) to your own PowerPoint slide and display it on your whiteboard. Alternatively, enlarge the image, laminate it and display it in your room, ready for use.

<u>When do I use it...?</u> Keep referring the 'engaging' to create the link between "active engagement and active learning" in lessons.

The 'Engaging' plenary image (above) is a powerful way of students evaluating their current level of engaging.

The plenary image also helps students to build a 'language of engaging'.

If you look at the image (above), you'll notice that the sentences inside the boxes are incomplete.

The idea is that students decide where they are then complete the sentence to articulate their current level of engaging.

The benefit of the plenary slide is that students need to communicate their understanding and, therefore, are beginning to become more aware of the importance of "active engagement to active learning".

When do I use it...? Use the 'Engaging: plenary' image in your lesson-plenary to review the skill.

## Praise

value

Praise is the ability to value someone and
not feel this devalues you.

Praise *validates* people and builds their
self-esteem.

Praise helps to maintain a person's
confidence and, if used enough, gives
people the courage to overcome obstacles.

The explanation image (above) on 'Praise' is designed for 'big picture' learners.

'Big picture' learners are concrete thinkers who need to able to visualise an idea in a practical situation.

The explanation for 'Praise' (above) paints a picture of what praise 'looks like' in the classroom.

How do I use it...? Convert the image (above) to your own PowerPoint slide and display it on your whiteboard. Alternatively, enlarge the image, laminate it and display it in your room, ready for use.

When do I use it...? Think about using the explanation image as your starter to help students make the connection between praise and motivation in lessons.

The '3 modes' image (above) is like holding up a mirror for your students and helping them to reflect on their current level of praise.

The small coloured boxes on the right-hand side highlight whether a student is in active, active-passive or passive mode. The use of these three modes helps students to see the impact of their level of praise on their active learning and behaviour in lessons.

How do I use it...? Convert the image (above) to your own PowerPoint slide and display it on your whiteboard. Alternatively, enlarge the image, laminate it and display it in your room, ready for use.

When do I use it...? Use the '3 modes' image during your lesson to re-establish students' understanding of the link between praise and motivation in lessons.

Praise 'Tips'

value

Praise in and out of the classroom. Why...?
This helps to build relationships with
people about school 'things' and non-school 'things'.

Praise small things and praise regularly. Why...?
Because regular praise makes people feel regularly
valued. This is like giving people 'emotional oxygen'.

The 'Praise Tips' image (above) is a visual example of how to develop students' awareness of the link between praise and motivation in lessons.

This provides with concrete strategies they can start using in school and life.

How do I use it...? Convert the image (above) to your own PowerPoint slide and display it on your whiteboard. Alternatively, enlarge the image, laminate it and display it in your room, ready for use.

When do I use it...? Keep referring the 'praise' to create the link between praise, motivation and the desire to please.

**Praise**

plenary: reflection

Use the 'prompts' to talk about your mature use of praise

"I tried to use praise equally. I think this helped to make others..."
"I tried to pick on the people who needed private praise so that..."

Builds the relationship

Maturity
Effective

Use the 'prompts' to talk about your adolescent use of praise

"Looking back, I think I praised the confident students which..."
"I gave praise, but I'm not sure I praised consistently which..."

Confuses the relationship

Adolescence
Ineffective

Use the 'prompts' to talk about your immature use of praise

"I can see I only praised things that I valued myself which..."
"I ignored good ideas that weren't my own which must have..."

Damages the relationship

Destructive
Destructive

The 'Praise' plenary image (above) is a powerful way of students evaluating their current level of praise.

The plenary image also helps students to build a 'language of praise'.

If you look at the image (above), you'll notice that the sentences inside the boxes are incomplete.

The idea is that students decide where they are then complete the sentence to articulate their current level of praise.

The benefit of the plenary slide is that students need to communicate their understanding and, therefore, are beginning to become more aware of the link between praise and motivation in lessons.

When do I use it...? Use the 'Praise: plenary' image in your lesson-plenary to review the skill.

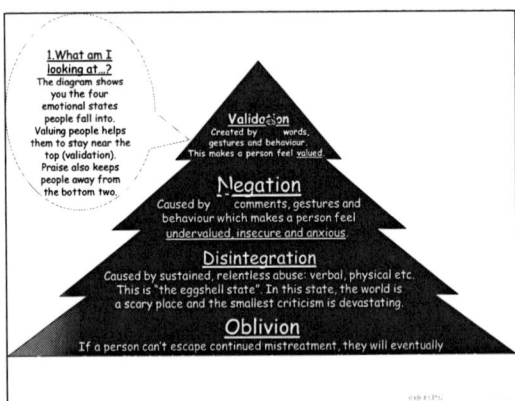

The image of 'The Mood Mountain' (above) is a visual representation of how our emotional intelligence and relationship-skills affects the mood of others.

<u>When would I use 'The Mood Mountain'...?</u>

Consider using 'The Mood Mountain' when students/classes are struggling with their behaviour. Poor behaviour is directly to poor empathy and, their poor emotional-and-social intelligence. 'The Mood Mountain' can improve students' emotional-and-social intelligence and, in turn, their behaviour.

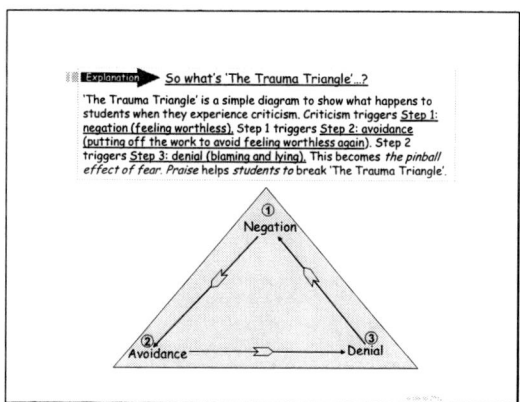

The image of 'The Trauma Triangle' (above) is a visual representation of the impact of criticism (i.e. negation) on a person's psychological and emotional state. This can help teachers and students to be more aware of the language they use when talking to others.

<u>When would I use 'The Trauma Triangle'...?</u>

Consider using 'The Trauma Triangle' when a relationship has broken-down with a student. 'The Trauma Triangle' can help you, the teacher, to reflect on a student's disengagement. Students disengage once they have experienced criticism (i.e. negation in the image above). Criticism is the entry into 'The Trauma Triangle'. Understanding this can help you, the teacher, to be more conscious of avoiding the use of negative with your students.

## The 4 Aspects of Relationships
an explanation

The 4 Aspects of Relationships covers four key
areas, all of which are important to develop and
maintain good relationships

The four areas are:
- The Operational (day-to-day routines)
- The Psychological (trauma and its impact)
- The Emotional (empathy, sensitivity, relativity)
- The Spiritual (reading gestures/moods/energy)

The image of 'The 4 Aspects of Relationships' (above) offers a deeper insight into how we relate to other people. People relate in one of four ways.

The next page gives an overview of 'The 4 Aspects of Relationships'.

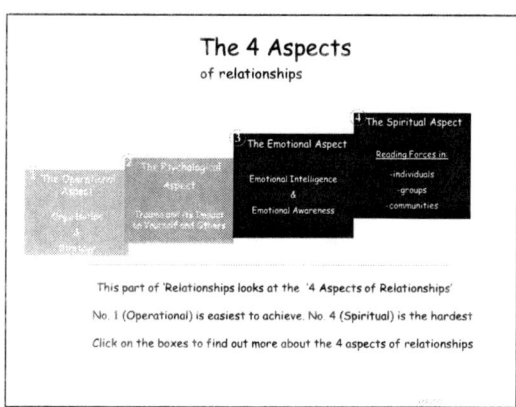

The image of 'The 4 Aspects of Relationships' (above) is the big picture of the four aspects.

The next page provides more detail on each of the aspects.

When would I need to use this...?

Consider reflecting on 'The 4 Aspects of Relationships' in relation to your own teaching. Which aspect are you in...? Are you happy with this aspect...? Do you think you may need some of the other aspects in certain situations...?

The '4 Aspects of Relationships' is a tool to help you reflect on your own teaching and how using different aspects at different times may help you.

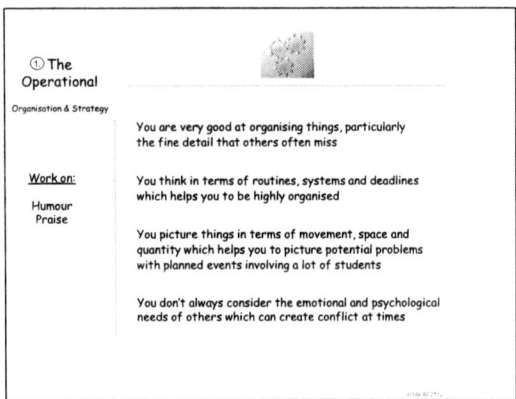

The image of 'The Operational Aspect' (above) is an explanation of the first of the four aspects.

How do I use these aspects of relationships...?

Once you've read the explanation, consider whether this reminds you of yourself. If it does, work on the two skills in the left-hand margin: i.e. humour, praise.

The next page gives an overview of 'The Psychological Phase'.

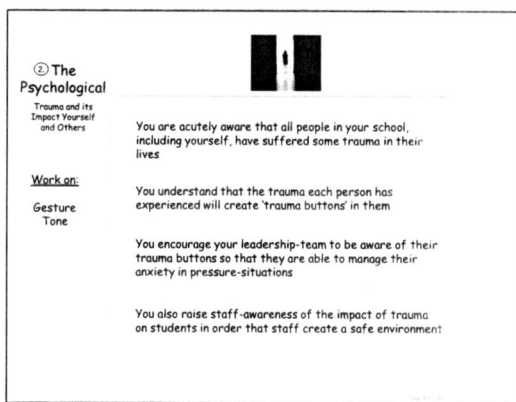

The image of 'The Psychological Aspect' (above) is an explanation of the second of the four aspects.

How do I use these aspects of relationships…?

Once you've read the explanation, consider whether this reminds you of yourself. If it does, work on the two skills in the left-hand margin: i.e. gesture, tone.

The next page gives an overview of 'The Emotional Phase'.

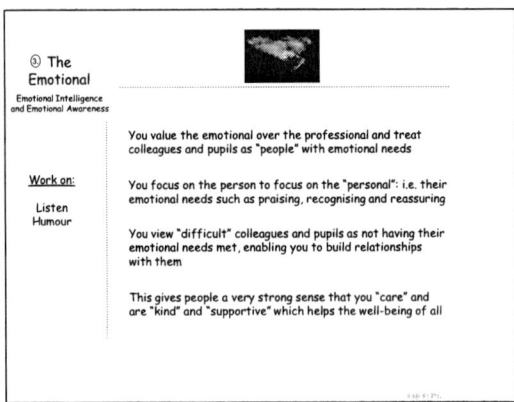

The image of 'The Emotional Aspect' (above) is an explanation of the third of the four aspects.

### How do I use these aspects of relationships...?

Once you've read the explanation, consider whether this reminds you of yourself. If it does, work on the two skills in the left-hand margin: i.e. listen, humour.

The next page gives an overview of 'The Spiritual Phase'.

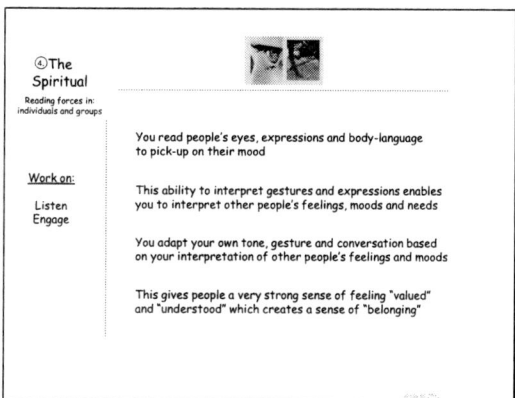

The image of 'The Spiritual Aspect' (above) is an explanation of the fourth of the four aspects.

<u>How do I use these aspects of relationships...?</u>

Once you've read the explanation, consider whether this reminds you of yourself. If it does, work on the two skills in the left-hand margin: i.e. listen, engage.

Element 3 - Motivation

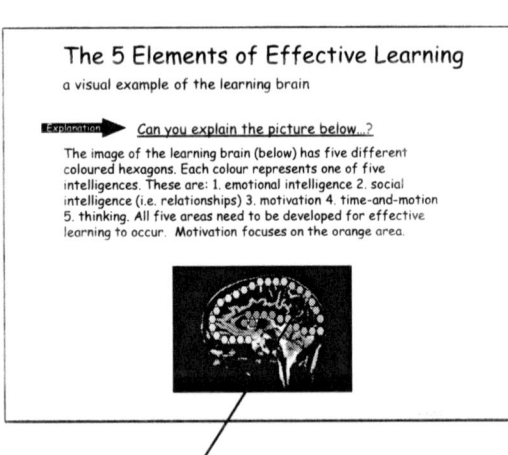

# The 5 Elements of Effective Learning
a visual example of the learning brain

Explanation ➤ Can you explain the picture below...?

The image of the learning brain (below) has five different coloured hexagons. Each colour represents one of five intelligences. These are: 1. emotional intelligence 2. social intelligence (i.e. relationships) 3. motivation 4. time-and-motion 5. thinking. All five areas need to be developed for effective learning to occur. Motivation focuses on the orange area.

'Motivation' is the third of the five elements. In the image above, motivation is represented by the third section in the learning brain. There are six hexagons because each area has six skills. The six skills for 'Motivation' are:

1.Desire    2.Drive    3.Resilience    4.Stamina    5.Confidence    6.Pride

## Why is 'Motivation' element three...?

Because once teachers and students have built positive relationships (i.e. relationship skills – element two), students feel more enthused and emotionally connected to the lessons. This enthusiasm and emotional investment makes the students more motivated to do well – for themselves and to regain the emotional connection with their teacher. This is why it's the third element.

The third section of the book is, therefore, on the six motivation skills.

You will see an image above each page, providing with a resource to go along with the skill.

### Desire
for success

Desire is having a clear idea/ 'picture' of what you want to be and how you're going to achieve it.

Desire is the *root of all success* because people with desire are driven to their goal.

Desire gives you a *clear path to follow* and *keeps you on that path*.

Internal Desire    You have *your own* goals/dreams.

External Desire    You live *someone else's* goals/dream.

The explanation image (above) on 'Desire' is designed for 'big picture' learners.

'Big picture' learners are concrete thinkers who need to able to visualise an idea in a practical situation.

The explanation for 'Desire' (above) paints a picture of what desire 'looks like' in the classroom.

How do I use it...? Convert the image (above) to your own PowerPoint slide and display it on your whiteboard. Alternatively, enlarge the image, laminate it and display it in your room, ready for use.

When do I use it...? Think about using the explanation image as your starter to help students make the connection between desire and success.

The '3 modes' image (above) is like holding up a mirror for your students and helping them to reflect on their current level of desire.

The small coloured boxes on the right-hand side highlight whether a student is in active, active-passive or passive mode. The use of these three modes helps students to see the impact of their level of desire on their performance and attitude in lessons.

How do I use it...? Convert the image (above) to your own PowerPoint slide and display it on your whiteboard. Alternatively, enlarge the image, laminate it and display it in your room, ready for use.

When do I use it...? Use the '3 modes' image during your lesson to re-establish students' need to 'focus on your future to perform now'.

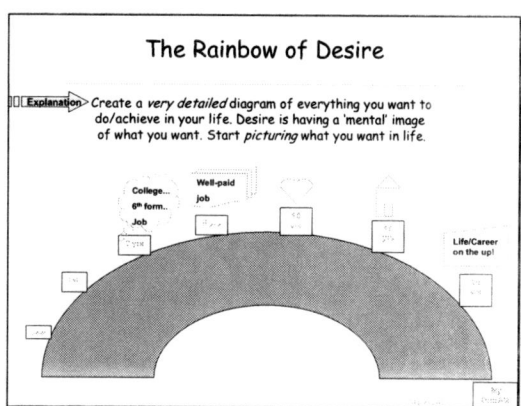

The 'Rainbow of Desire' image (above) is a visual example of how to set long-term goals.

This helps students to clearly see how to create their own 'Rainbow of Desire'.

How do I use it...? Convert the image (above) to your own PowerPoint slide and display it on your whiteboard. Alternatively, enlarge the image, laminate it and display it in your room, ready for use.

When do I use it...? Keep referring the 'Rainbow of Desire' image to sustain your classroom climate.

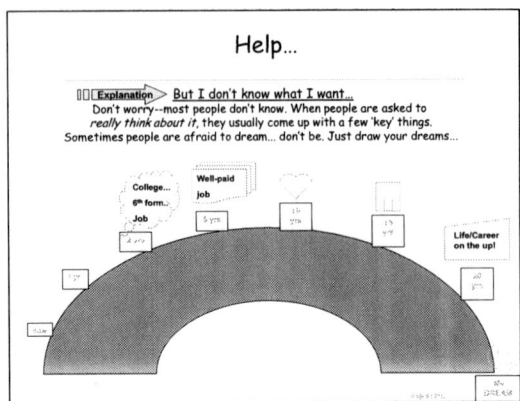

The 'Help' image (above) is further clarification on students set long-term goals.

Students often struggle with what to put on their own 'Rainbow of Desire'.

How do I use it...? Convert the image (above) to your own PowerPoint slide and display it on your whiteboard. Alternatively, enlarge the image, laminate it and display it in your room, ready for use.

When do I use it...? Use the 'help' image to reinforce to students that they are simply writing down and illustrating their hopes/dreams/ambitions.

The 'Desire' plenary image (above) is a powerful way of students evaluating their current level of desire.

The plenary image also helps students to build a 'language of desire'.

If you look at the image (above), you'll notice that the sentences inside the boxes are incomplete.

The idea is that students decide where they are then complete the sentence to articulate their current level of desire.

The benefit of the plenary slide is that students need to communicate their understanding and, therefore, are beginning to become more aware of the importance of setting long-term goals to success in school.

<u>When do I use it...?</u> Use the 'Desire: plenary' image in your lesson-plenary to review the skill.

**Drive**

focus

Drive comes from having a desire to achieve something.

Drive is knowing what you want and pushing yourself towards it.

| Internal Drive | You have a goal/plan which means your performance is high. |
| External Drive | You're driven by someone else's goal/plan so your performance is mixed. |

The explanation image (above) on 'Drive' is designed for 'big picture' learners.

'Big picture' learners are concrete thinkers who need to able to visualise an idea in a practical situation.

The explanation for 'Drive' (above) paints a picture of what drive (i.e. determination) 'looks like' in the classroom.

How do I use it...? Convert the image (above) to your own PowerPoint slide and display it on your whiteboard. Alternatively, enlarge the image, laminate it and display it in your room, ready for use.

When do I use it...? Think about using the explanation image as your starter to help students make the connection between drive (i.e. determination) and success.

The '3 modes' image (above) is like holding up a mirror for your students and helping them to reflect on their current level of drive (i.e. determination).

The small coloured boxes on the right-hand side highlight whether a student is in active, active-passive or passive mode. The use of these three modes helps students to see the impact of their level of drive on their performance and attitude in lessons.

How do I use it...? Convert the image (above) to your own PowerPoint slide and display it on your whiteboard. Alternatively, enlarge the image, laminate it and display it in your room, ready for use.

When do I use it...? Use the '3 modes' image during your lesson to re-establish students' need to 'focus on your future to perform now'.

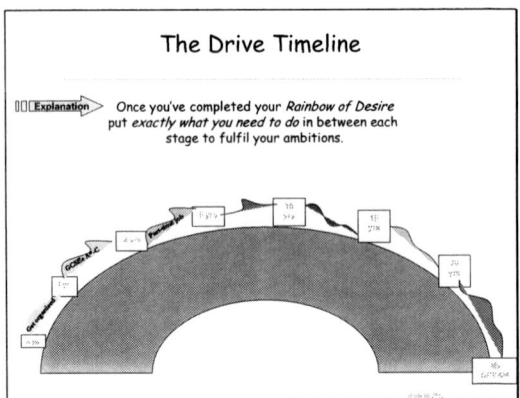

The 'Drive Timeline' image (above) is a visual example of clarifying the factors required to achieve long-term goals.

This helps students to understand the how 'Drive' is formed within people.

How do I use it...? Convert the image (above) to your own PowerPoint slide and display it on your whiteboard. Alternatively, enlarge the image, laminate it and display it in your room, ready for use.

When do I use it...? Use the 'Help' slide when you are focusing on raising aspirations and setting short/mid-term goals.

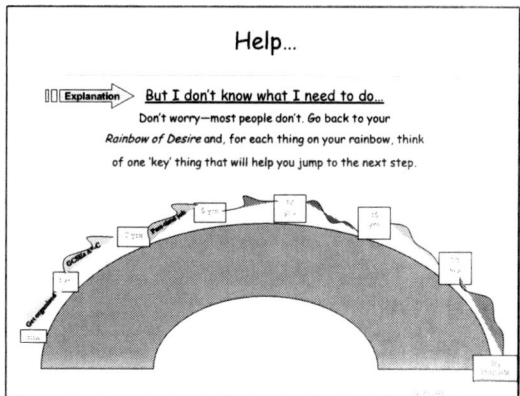

The 'Help' image for the 'Drive Timeline' image (above) provides further clarity on how to set mid/short-term goals.

This helps students to understand how to create their own 'Drive Timeline'.

How do I use it...? Convert the image (above) to your own PowerPoint slide and display it on your whiteboard. Alternatively, enlarge the image, laminate it and display it in your room, ready for use.

When do I use it...? Use the 'Help' image if your students are uncertain of what to include in their 'Drive Timeline'.

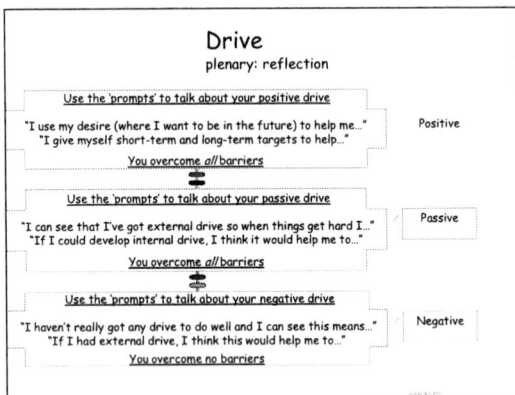

The 'Drive' plenary image (above) is a powerful way of students evaluating their current level of drive.

The plenary image also helps students to build a 'language of drive'.

If you look at the image (above), you'll notice that the sentences inside the boxes are incomplete.

The idea is that students decide where they are then complete the sentence to articulate their current level of drive.

The benefit of the plenary slide is that students need to communicate their understanding and, therefore, are beginning to become more aware of the importance of setting short/mid-term goals to success in school.

When do I use it...? Use the 'Drive: plenary' image in your lesson-plenary to review the skill.

**Resilience**
"I will"

Resilience is *refusing to give up*. Resilience is a mixture of pride and a determaination *not to give in*.

Resilience can be built by *realising that everyone struggles sometimes* because all learning is *trial-and-error*. Resilience is knowing that it's those that carry on ("I will") who succeed.

The explanation image (above) on 'Resilience' is designed for 'big picture' learners.

'Big picture' learners are concrete thinkers who need to able to visualise an idea in a practical situation.

The explanation for 'Resilience' (above) paints a picture of what resilience (i.e. mental strength) 'looks like' in the classroom.

How do I use it...? Convert the image (above) to your own PowerPoint slide and display it on your whiteboard. Alternatively, enlarge the image, laminate it and display it in your room, ready for use.

When do I use it...? Think about using the explanation image as your starter to help students make the connection between resilience (i.e. mental strength) and success.

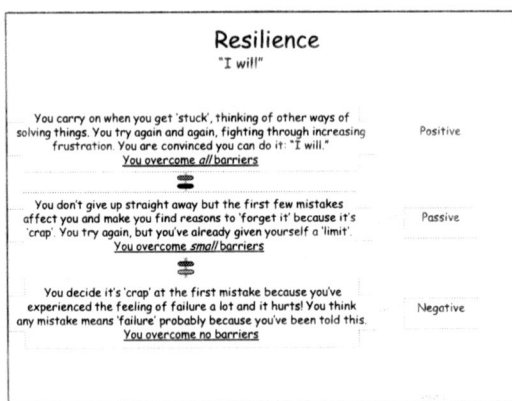

The '3 modes' image (above) is like holding up a mirror for your students and helping them to reflect on their current level of resilience (i.e. mental strength).

The small coloured boxes on the right-hand side highlight whether a student is in active, active-passive or passive mode. The use of these three modes helps students to see the impact of their level of resilience on their performance and attitude in lessons.

How do I use it...? Convert the image (above) to your own PowerPoint slide and display it on your whiteboard. Alternatively, enlarge the image, laminate it and display it in your room, ready for use.

When do I use it...? Use the '3 modes' image during your lesson to re-establish students' need to have the mental strength and flexibility to overcome learning obstacles.

The 'Resilience: mantra' image (above) is a simple strategy to help students overcome their self-limiting beliefs.

This helps students to understand how people will a resilient mindset think.

<u>How do I use it...?</u> Convert the image (above) to your own PowerPoint slide and display it on your whiteboard. Alternatively, enlarge the image, laminate it and display it in your room, ready for use.

<u>When do I use it...?</u> Use the 'mantra' slide when you are focusing on developing resilience and the idea of 'stickability' with your students.

The 'Resilience' plenary image (above) is a powerful way of students evaluating their current level of resilience.

The plenary image also helps students to build a 'language of resilience'.

If you look at the image (above), you'll notice that the sentences inside the boxes are incomplete.

The idea is that students decide where they are then complete the sentence to articulate their current level of resilience.

The benefit of the plenary slide is that students need to communicate their understanding and, therefore, are beginning to become more aware of the importance of overcoming self-limiting beliefs in order to be successful.

When do I use it...? Use the 'Resilience: plenary' image in your lesson-plenary to review the skill.

**Stamina**

reserves

Stamina is having *reserves*. Stamina helps you to carry on when you start to struggle or get tired. Stamina is crucial to success because all learning *involves* *struggling, frustration and tiredness.*

You can build your stamina *(reserves)* by thinking: "I can" (Confidence), "I will" (Resilience), "I am" (Pride).

The explanation image (above) on 'Stamina' is designed for 'big picture' learners.

'Big picture' learners are concrete thinkers who need to able to visualise an idea in a practical situation.

The explanation for 'Stamina' (above) paints a picture of what stamina (i.e. mental reserves) 'looks like' in the classroom.

How do I use it...? Convert the image (above) to your own PowerPoint slide and display it on your whiteboard. Alternatively, enlarge the image, laminate it and display it in your room, ready for use.

When do I use it...? Think about using the explanation image as your starter to help students make the connection between stamina (i.e. mental reserves) and success.

**Stamina**
reserves

| | |
|---|---|
| You understand that struggling, getting it wrong and getting annoyed is part of learning. This helps you to "continue". You've also learnt that by "struggling" you always "get there in the end." You overcome *all* barriers | Positive |
| You have some stamina because you fight the early signs of frustration and confusion. Your mindset soon changes from "I can" to "Can I?" and you begin to think of other things to do. You overcome *some* barriers | Passive |
| You have no stamina because you get angry at the first problem. You don't realise that struggling and getting it wrong is something *everyone goes through*. You see a mistake as failure. You overcome no barriers | Negative |

The '3 modes' image (above) is like holding up a mirror for your students and helping them to reflect on their current level of stamina (i.e. mental reserves).

The small coloured boxes on the right-hand side highlight whether a student is in active, active-passive or passive mode. The use of these three modes helps students to see the impact of their level of stamina on their performance and attitude in lessons.

How do I use it...? Convert the image (above) to your own PowerPoint slide and display it on your whiteboard. Alternatively, enlarge the image, laminate it and display it in your room, ready for use.

When do I use it...? Use the '3 modes' image during your lesson to re-establish students' need to have the mental reserves to be consistent, high-achieving learners.

The 'Stamina: mantra' image (above) is a simple strategy to help students to develop 'mental reserves'.

<u>How do I use it...?</u>  Convert the image (above) to your own PowerPoint slide and display it on your whiteboard. Alternatively, enlarge the image, laminate it and display it in your room, ready for use.

<u>When do I use it...?</u> Use the 'mantra' slide when you are focusing on developing students' awareness of and ability to draw on their 'mental reserves'.

**Stamina**
plenary: reflection

Use the 'prompts' to talk about your positive state of stamina

"I know that struggling is part of learning so I don't give up when..."
"I'm more tired at the end of the day so I change the way I..."          Positive

You overcome *all* barriers

Use the 'prompts' to talk about your passive state of stamina          Passive

"I can see that I give up after I've tried for a bit instead of..."
"Now I know that struggling is part of getting better, I'm going to..."

You overcome *some* barriers

Use the 'prompts' to talk about your negative state of stamina          Negative

"I get wound-up as soon as I make a mistake which ends up in..."
"Now I know that mistakes are normal, I won't be so scared of..."

You overcome no barriers

The 'Stamina' plenary image (above) is a powerful way of students evaluating their current level of stamina.

The plenary image also helps students to build a 'language of stamina'.

If you look at the image (above), you'll notice that the sentences inside the boxes are incomplete.

The idea is that students decide where they are then complete the sentence to articulate their current level of stamina.

The benefit of the plenary slide is that students need to communicate their understanding and, therefore, are beginning to become more aware of the importance of developing 'mental reserves' for success.

When do I use it...? Use the 'Stamina: plenary' image in your lesson-plenary to review the skill.

**Confidence**
"I can"

Confidence is a state of mind. People are often held back because of a lack of confidence. This means that people often don't reach their potential.

Turning 'Can I?' into 'I can' is one of the simplest ways of getting a Positive Mental Attitude. Believing 'I can' improves your resilience and stamina.

The explanation image (above) on 'Confidence' is designed for 'big picture' learners.

'Big picture' learners are concrete thinkers who need to able to visualise an idea in a practical situation.

The explanation for 'Confidence' (above) paints a picture of what confidence (i.e. a positive mental attitude) 'looks like' in the classroom.

How do I use it...? Convert the image (above) to your own PowerPoint slide and display it on your whiteboard. Alternatively, enlarge the image, laminate it and display it in your room, ready for use.

When do I use it...? Think about using the explanation image as your starter to help students make the connection between confidence (i.e. a positive mental attitude) and success.

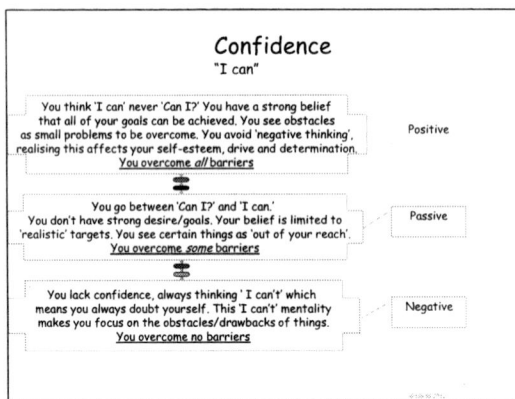

The '3 modes' image (above) is like holding up a mirror for your students and helping them to reflect on their current level of confidence (i.e. a positive mental attitude).

The small coloured boxes on the right-hand side highlight whether a student is in active, active-passive or passive mode. The use of these three modes helps students to see the impact of their level of confidence on their performance and attitude in lessons.

How do I use it...? Convert the image (above) to your own PowerPoint slide and display it on your whiteboard. Alternatively, enlarge the image, laminate it and display it in your room, ready for use.

When do I use it...? Use the '3 modes' image during your lesson to re-establish students' need to have a positive mental attitude to overcome obstacles and reach their potential.

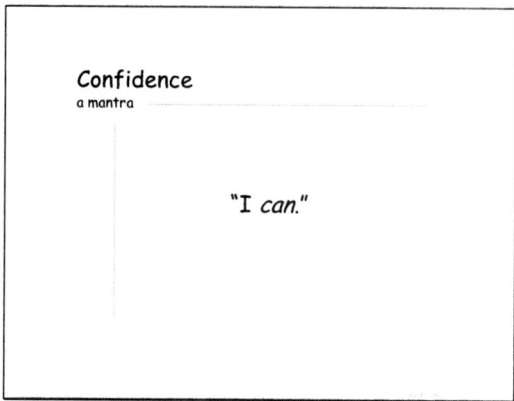

The 'Confidence: mantra' image (above) is a simple strategy to help students to develop a positive mental attitude.

How do I use it...? Convert the image (above) to your own PowerPoint slide and display it on your whiteboard. Alternatively, enlarge the image, laminate it and display it in your room, ready for use.

When do I use it...? Use the 'mantra' slide when you are focusing on developing students' awareness of the need to have a positive mental attitude in order to reach their potential.

# Confidence
### plenary: reflection

Use the 'prompts' to talk about your positive state of confidence

"I think "I can" which builds my resilience and stamina, helping me to..."
"I avoid negative thinking because I know it will affect the way I..."

You overcome *all* barriers

Positive

Use the 'prompts' to talk about your passive state of confidence

"I can see that I think "Can I...?" which makes me doubt myself and..."
"If I can turn "Can I...?" into "I can", it would build my resilience and..."

You overcome *some* barriers

Passive

Use the 'prompts' to talk about your negative state of confidence

"I can see that I think "I can't" which stops me taking risks so I..."
"I need to start saying "I can" to myself which will help me to..."

You overcome no barriers

Negative

The 'Confidence' plenary image (above) is a powerful way of students evaluating their current level of confidence.

The plenary image also helps students to build a 'language of confidence'.

If you look at the image (above), you'll notice that the sentences inside the boxes are incomplete.

The idea is that students decide where they are then complete the sentence to articulate their current level of confidence.

The benefit of the plenary slide is that students need to communicate their understanding and, therefore, are beginning to become more aware of the importance of developing a positive mental attitude for success.

<u>When do I use it...?</u>  Use the 'Confidence: plenary' image in your lesson-plenary to review the skill.

Pride
"I am"

Pride is having an "I'm worth it" attitude.
Sometimes people don't go for what they
really want because they think it's "out of
their league".

Thinking "I'm worth it" builds your sense of
pride which makes you believe that *everything
is in your reach*. Pride is believing in yourself:
"I am."

The explanation image (above) on 'Pride' is designed for 'big picture' learners.

'Big picture' learners are concrete thinkers who need to able to visualise an idea in a practical situation.

The explanation for 'Pride' (above) paints a picture of what pride (i.e. a positive self-image) 'looks like' in the classroom.

How do I use it…? Convert the image (above) to your own PowerPoint slide and display it on your whiteboard. Alternatively, enlarge the image, laminate it and display it in your room, ready for use.

When do I use it…? Think about using the explanation image as your starter to help students make the connection between pride (i.e. a positive self-image) and success.

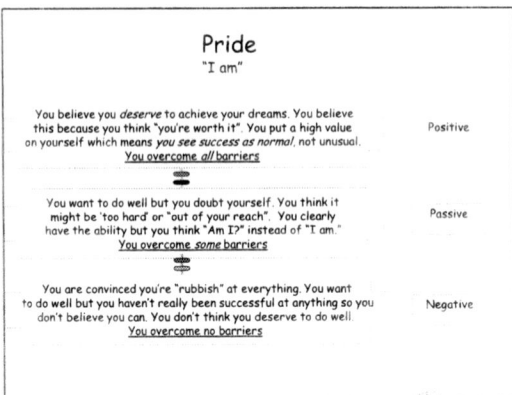

The '3 modes' image (above) is like holding up a mirror for your students and helping them to reflect on their current level of pride (i.e. a positive self-image).

The small coloured boxes on the right-hand side highlight whether a student is in active, active-passive or passive mode. The use of these three modes helps students to see the impact of their level of pride on their performance and attitude in lessons.

How do I use it...? Convert the image (above) to your own PowerPoint slide and display it on your whiteboard. Alternatively, enlarge the image, laminate it and display it in your room, ready for use.

When do I use it...? Use the '3 modes' image during your lesson to re-establish students' need to have a positive self-image to overcome obstacles and reach their potential.

```
+------------------------------------------------+
|                                                |
|   Pride                                         |
|   a mantra        _____       |
|                                                |
|                                                |
|                     "I am."                     |
|                                                |
|                                                |
|                                                |
|                                                |
+------------------------------------------------+
```

The 'Pride: mantra' image (above) is a simple strategy to help students to develop a positive self-image.

How do I use it...? Convert the image (above) to your own PowerPoint slide and display it on your whiteboard. Alternatively, enlarge the image, laminate it and display it in your room, ready for use.

When do I use it...? Use the 'mantra' slide when you are focusing on developing students' awareness of the need to have a positive self-image in order to reach their potential.

Pride
plenary: reflection

Use the 'prompts' to help you talk about your positive state of pride | Positive

"I realise that I see doing well as normal... I believe I can do well which..."
"I also think I deserve to do well if I put the effort in ... This helps to..."

You overcome *all* barriers

Use the 'prompts' to talk about your passive state of pride | Passive

"I doubt myself, thinking "Am I?" instead "I am" ... This means I..."
"If I can stop seeing things as "out of my league", I'll be able to..."

You overcome *some* barriers

Use the 'prompts' to talk about your negative state of pride | Negative

"I can see that I don't really value myself that much which means I..."
"If I can start thinking "I am" instead of "I'm not", it will help me to..."

You overcome no barriers

The 'Pride' plenary image (above) is a powerful way of students evaluating their current level of pride.

The plenary image also helps students to build a 'language of pride'.

If you look at the image (above), you'll notice that the sentences inside the boxes are incomplete.

The idea is that students decide where they are then complete the sentence to articulate their current level of pride.

The benefit of the plenary slide is that students need to communicate their understanding and, therefore, are beginning to become more aware of the importance of developing a positive self-image for success.

When do I use it...? Use the 'Pride: plenary' image in your lesson-plenary to review the skill.

Element 4 – Time-and-Motion

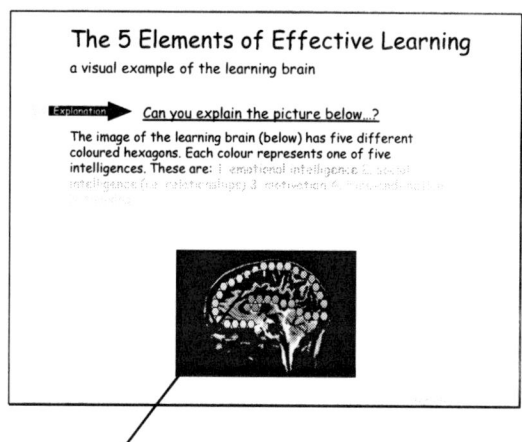

'Time-and-Motion' is the fourth of the five elements. In the image above, time-and-motion is represented by the fourth section in the learning brain. There are six hexagons because each area has six skills. The six skills for 'Time-and-motion' are:

1.Operating   2.Arriving   3.Organising   4.Recording   5.Revising   6.Performing

Why is 'Time-and-motion' element three...?

Because once students feel more enthused and emotionally connected to the lessons (i.e. motivation – element three), they will begin to turn up early to lessons, operate better, be more organised, spend more time on revision and perform at a higher level. This is because students now have an emotional investment in the lesson and the school. This emotional investment is directly related to their internal motivation created by the positive relationships built up by the teacher. This is why it's the third element.

The third section of the book is, therefore, on the six time-and-motion skills.

You will see an image above each page, providing with a resource to go along with the skill.

> ## Operating
> in class
>
> *Operating in class* is the skill of *staying focused* and 'on task' when you're working independently.
>
> A lot of students see learning as 'being told' so when the teacher stops explaining, students see this as 'talk time'.
>
> *Operating in class* is understanding that you learn the most *on your own—thinking and re-working* things until you 'get it'.

The explanation image (above) on 'Operating-in-class' is designed for 'big picture' learners.

'Big picture' learners are concrete thinkers who need to able to visualise an idea in a practical situation.

The explanation for 'Operating-in-class' (above) paints a picture of what operating 'looks like' in the classroom.

How do I use it...? Convert the image (above) to your own PowerPoint slide and display it on your whiteboard. Alternatively, enlarge the image, laminate it and display it in your room, ready for use.

When do I use it...? Think about using the explanation image as your starter, to establish your climate.

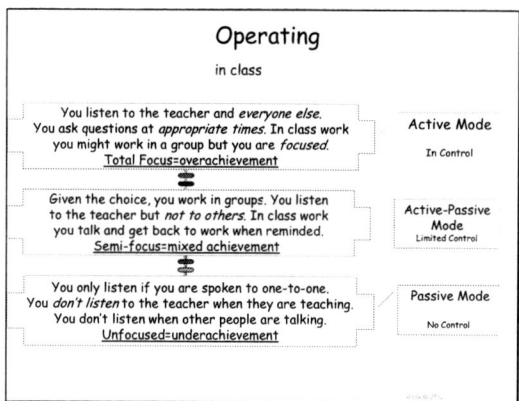

The '3 modes' image (above) is like holding up a mirror for your students and helping them to reflect on their current operation in class.

The small coloured boxes on the right-hand side highlight whether a student is in active, active-passive or passive mode. The use of these three modes helps students to see the impact of their operation.

How do I use it...? Convert the image (above) to your own PowerPoint slide and display it on your whiteboard. Alternatively, enlarge the image, laminate it and display it in your room, ready for use.

When do I use it...? Use the '3 modes' image during your lesson, to re-establish your climate.

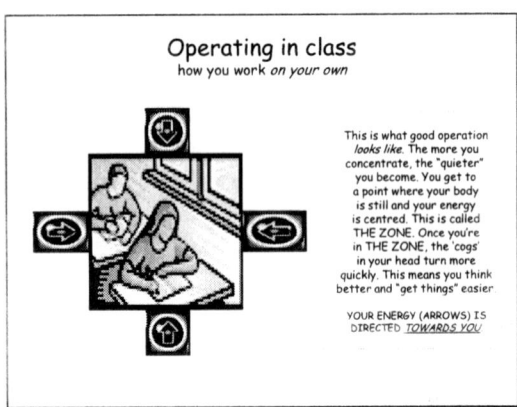

The 'Good Operation' image (above) is a visual example of what good operation looks like.

This helps students to clearly see what's expected of them. You can reinforce this with statements like: "body still, head down".

The arrows represent internal concentration.

How do I use it...? Convert the image (above) to your own PowerPoint slide and display it on your whiteboard. Alternatively, enlarge the image, laminate it and display it in your room, ready for use.

When do I use it...? Keep referring the 'Good Operation' image to sustain your classroom climate.

The 'Operating in class' plenary image (above) is a powerful way of students evaluating their current level of operation.

The plenary image also helps students to build a 'language of operation'.

If you look at the image (above), you'll notice that the sentences inside the boxes are incomplete.

The idea is that students decide where they are then complete the sentence to articulate their current level of operation.

The benefit of the plenary slide is that students need to communicate their understanding and, therefore, are beginning to become more aware of the importance of operation to success in school.

How do I use it...? Convert the image (above) to your own PowerPoint slide and display it on your whiteboard. Alternatively, enlarge the image, laminate it and display it in your room, ready for use.

When do I use it...? Use the 'Operating: plenary' image to help students link operating to behaviour.

## Arriving

to class

Being *on time* is the first sign you give to people about how much you care about them.

Being *on time* is a simple way of showing *respect* and *sensitivity* to other people.

Being *late* immediately lowers the mood of the person who is waiting for you.

The explanation image (above) on 'Arriving' is designed for 'big picture' learners.

'Big picture' learners are concrete thinkers who need to able to visualise an idea in a practical situation.

The explanation for 'Arriving' (above) paints a picture of what arriving 'looks like' in school.

How do I use it...? Convert the image (above) to your own PowerPoint slide and display it on your whiteboard. Alternatively, enlarge the image, laminate it and display it in your room, ready for use.

When do I use it...? Think about using the explanation image as your starter, to establish your climate.

**Arriving**

to class

| | |
|---|---|
| You arrive *early* or *on time* and are *fully organised.* You get books and folders out without being asked. <u>Total Focus=overachievement</u> | **Active Mode** <br> In Control |
| You arrive a *few minutes late* and are semi-organised. You are likely to have *forgotten something.* You wait for instructions before you start. <u>Semi-Focus=mixed achievement</u> | **Active-Passive Mode** <br> Limited Control |
| You arrive *very late* and are *unorganised.* You spend the first five minutes *talking/gazing* into space. You *almost always forget to bring something.* Unfocused=underachievement | **Passive Mode** <br> No Control |

The '3 modes' image (above) is like holding up a mirror for your students and helping them to reflect on their current level of arriving.

The small coloured boxes on the right-hand side highlight whether a student is in active, active-passive or passive mode. The use of these three modes helps students to see the impact of their current level of arriving to their learning.

<u>How do I use it...?</u> Convert the image (above) to your own PowerPoint slide and display it on your whiteboard. Alternatively, enlarge the image, laminate it and display it in your room, ready for use.

<u>When do I use it...?</u> Use the '3 modes' image at the beginning of your lesson to establish your climate.

The 'Good Arriver' image (above) is an example of the elements of effective arrival to lessons.

This helps students to clearly see what's expected of them. You can reinforce this with statements like: "look at good arrive explanation and do what it says".

How do I use it...? Convert the image (above) to your own PowerPoint slide and display it on your whiteboard. Alternatively, enlarge the image, laminate it and display it in your room, ready for use.

When do I use it...? Use the 'Good Arriver' image as a regular starter to sustain your classroom climate.

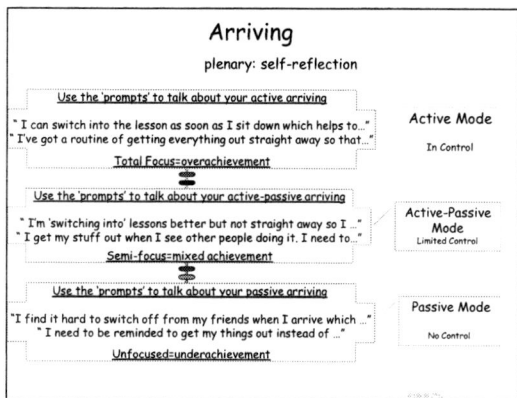

The 'Arriving' plenary image (above) is a powerful way of students evaluating their current level of arriving to lessons.

The plenary image also helps students to build a 'language of arriving'.

If you look at the image (above), you'll notice that the sentences inside the boxes are incomplete.

The idea is that students decide where they are then complete the sentence to articulate their current level of arriving.

The benefit of the plenary slide is that students need to communicate their understanding and, therefore, are beginning to become more aware of the importance of arriving to success in school.

How do I use it...? Convert the image (above) to your own PowerPoint slide and display it on your whiteboard. Alternatively, enlarge the image, laminate it and display it in your room, ready for use.

When do I use it...? Use the 'Arriving: plenary' image to help students link arriving to behaviour.

## Organising

your work

The time-and-motion skill of being *organised* can make a real difference to how well you learn.

*Organising* your work *organises your mind.* This helps you to see the *order* that you've learnt things in.

*Organising* your work into sections (with file dividers) helps you to see each 'piece' and how they link together.

The explanation image (above) on 'Organising' is designed for 'big picture' learners.

'Big picture' learners are concrete thinkers who need to able to visualise an idea in a practical situation.

The explanation for 'Organising' (above) paints a picture of what organisation 'looks like' in school.

How do I use it...? Convert the image (above) to your own PowerPoint slide and display it on your whiteboard. Alternatively, enlarge the image, laminate it and display it in your room, ready for use.

When do I use it...? Think about using the explanation image as your starter when you are focusing on the importance of organising to successful learning.

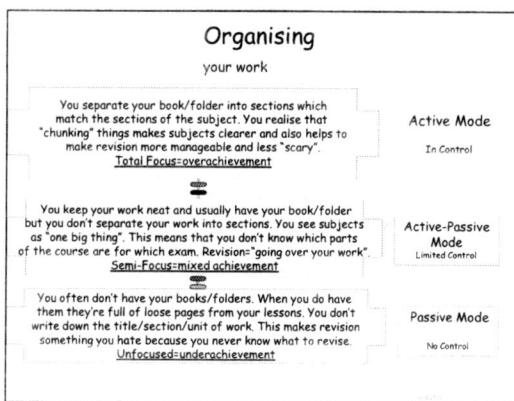

The '3 modes' image on 'Organising your Work' (above) is like holding up a mirror for your students and helping them to reflect on their current level of organisation.

The small coloured boxes on the right-hand side highlight whether a student is in active, active-passive or passive mode. The use of these three modes helps students to see the impact of their current level of organisation to their learning.

How do I use it...? Convert the image (above) to your own PowerPoint slide and display it on your whiteboard. Alternatively, enlarge the image, laminate it and display it in your room, ready for use.

When do I use it...? Use the '3 modes' image when you are having a specific focus on organisation.

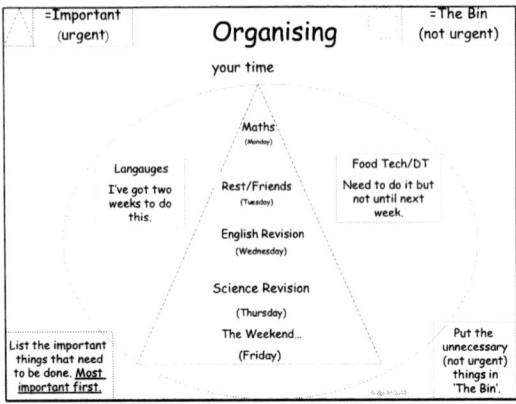

The 'Organising your Time' image (above) is a practical example of time-management.

This helps students to manage their workload more effectively and independently.

How do I use it...? Convert the image (above) to your own PowerPoint slide and display it on your whiteboard. Alternatively, enlarge the image, laminate it and display it in your room, ready for use.

When do I use it...? Use the 'Organising your Time' image as a regular starter when you are focusing on organisation.

**Organising** yourself

| | |
|---|---|
| You check your planner in the evening to make sure you've got the right books and equipment for the next day. You also check homework for that evening. You double-check just to make sure. *Total Focus=overachievement* | Active Mode *In Control* |
| You check your bag as you're leaving the house but you don't check your planner because you rely on your memory. This means you forget things, particularly when changes to the normal day have been made. You don't double-check to avoid mistakes. *Semi-Focus=mixed achievement* | Active-Passive Mode *Limited Control* |
| You might check your bag but this will be done when you're half-way to school or waiting at the bus-stop. You check for "the basics": pen, books. You don't think a planner is important. *Unfocused=underachievement* | Passive Mode *No Control* |

The '3 modes' image on 'Organising Yourself' (above) is an additional organisation slide, helping them to reflect on their current level of organisation.

The small coloured boxes on the right-hand side highlight whether a student is in active, active-passive or passive mode. The use of these three modes helps students to see the impact of their current level of organisation to their learning.

How do I use it...? Convert the image (above) to your own PowerPoint slide and display it on your whiteboard. Alternatively, enlarge the image, laminate it and display it in your room, ready for use.

When do I use it...? Use the '3 modes' image when you are having a specific focus on organisation

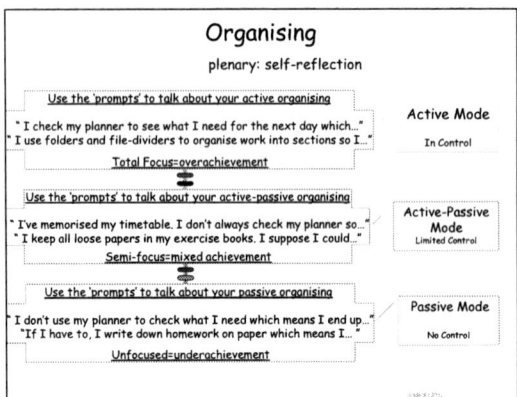

The 'Organising' plenary image (above) is a powerful way of students evaluating their current level of organisation.

The plenary image also helps students to build a 'language of organisation'.

If you look at the image (above), you'll notice that the sentences inside the boxes are incomplete.

The idea is that students decide where they are then complete the sentence to articulate their current level of organisation.

The benefit of the plenary slide is that students need to communicate their understanding and, therefore, are beginning to become more aware of the importance of organisation to success in school.

How do I use it...? Convert the image (above) to your own PowerPoint slide and display it on your whiteboard. Alternatively, enlarge the image, laminate it and display it in your room, ready for use.

When do I use it...? Use the 'Organising: plenary' image to help students link organisation to successful learning.

## Recording

homework

Recording independent study accurately and precisely is an important time-and-motion skill.

The importance of recording independent study *word-for-word* helps you to include the *most important points*.

Also, writing *your own deadline* teaches you to manage your time.

The explanation image (above) on 'Recording' is designed for 'big picture' learners.

'Big picture' learners are concrete thinkers who need to able to visualise an idea in a practical situation.

The explanation for 'Recording' (above) paints a picture of what recording 'looks like' in school.

How do I use it...? Convert the image (above) to your own PowerPoint slide and display it on your whiteboard. Alternatively, enlarge the image, laminate it and display it in your room, ready for use.

When do I use it...? Think about using the explanation image as your starter when you are focusing on the importance of recording information effectively.

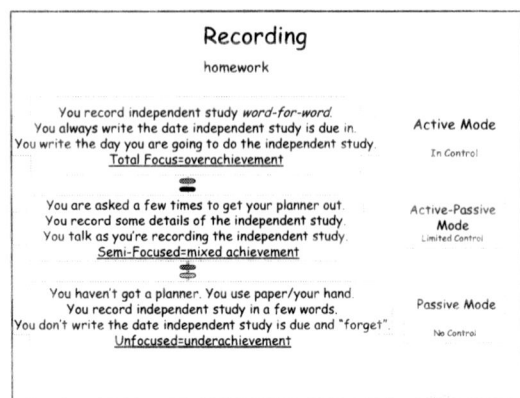

The '3 modes' image on 'Recording Information' (above) is like holding up a mirror for your students and helping them to reflect on their current level of recording.

The small coloured boxes on the right-hand side highlight whether a student is in active, active-passive or passive mode. The use of these three modes helps students to see the impact of their current level of recording information.

How do I use it...? Convert the image (above) to your own PowerPoint slide and display it on your whiteboard. Alternatively, enlarge the image, laminate it and display it in your room, ready for use.

When do I use it...? Use the '3 modes' image when you are having a specific focus on recording information.

The Good Recorder

**Active Mode**
In Control

You focus on the teacher and the board when independent study is being set.

You record independent study *word-for-word* because you know that missing out words=missing out key points in your independent study.

You record the deadline set + *your own deadline*. Recording *your own deadline* helps you to mentally 'block' the time you're going to do it.

The 'Good Recorder' image (above) is a visual reinforcement of how to record information effectively to lessons.

This helps students to clearly see what's expected of them. You can reinforce this with statements like: "colour-code/underline key instruction words".

How do I use it...? Convert the image (above) to your own PowerPoint slide and display it on your whiteboard. Alternatively, enlarge the image, laminate it and display it in your room, ready for use.

When do I use it...? Use the 'Good Recorder' image when you're setting homework, particularly with younger students, to reinforce how to record information effectively.

The 'Recording' plenary image (above) is a powerful way of students evaluating their current level of recording information effectively.

The plenary image also helps students to build a 'language of recording'.

If you look at the image (above), you'll notice that the sentences inside the boxes are incomplete.

The idea is that students decide where they are then complete the sentence to articulate their current level of recording.

The benefit of the plenary slide is that students need to communicate their understanding and, therefore, are beginning to become more aware of the importance of recording information effectively to success in school.

How do I use it...? Convert the image (above) to your own PowerPoint slide and display it on your whiteboard. Alternatively, enlarge the image, laminate it and display it in your room, ready for use.

When do I use it...? Use the 'Recording: plenary' image to help students link recording information effectively to successful learning.

**Revising**

for exams

Revising for exams often causes stress and anxiety. You often don't know where to start.

It feels like you've got too many subjects to revise and too much to revise in every subject.

The skill of *revising* is underestimated. It isn't just looking through your books. To revise well you need to *"block"* your free-time and *"revise"* your *focus* subjects.

The explanation image (above) on 'Revising' is designed for 'big picture' learners.

'Big picture' learners are concrete thinkers who need to able to visualise an idea in a practical situation.

The explanation for 'Revising' (above) paints a picture of what recording 'looks like' in school.

How do I use it...? Convert the image (above) to your own PowerPoint slide and display it on your whiteboard. Alternatively, enlarge the image, laminate it and display it in your room, ready for use.

When do I use it...? Think about using the explanation image as your starter when you are focusing on the importance of revising.

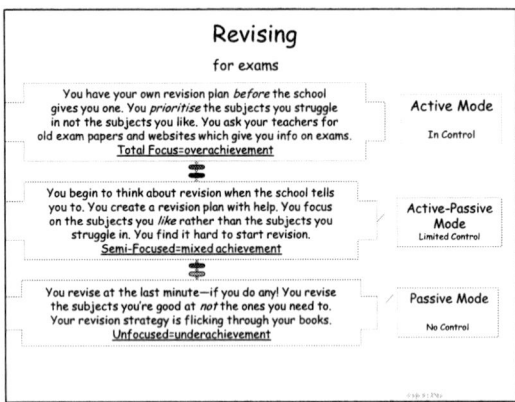

The '3 modes' image on 'Revising' (above) is like holding up a mirror for your students and helping them to reflect on their current level of revision.

The small coloured boxes on the right-hand side highlight whether a student is in active, active-passive or passive mode. The use of these three modes helps students to see the impact of their current level of revision.

How do I use it...? Convert the image (above) to your own PowerPoint slide and display it on your whiteboard. Alternatively, enlarge the image, laminate it and display it in your room, ready for use.

When do I use it...? Use the '3 modes' image when you are having a specific focus on revision.

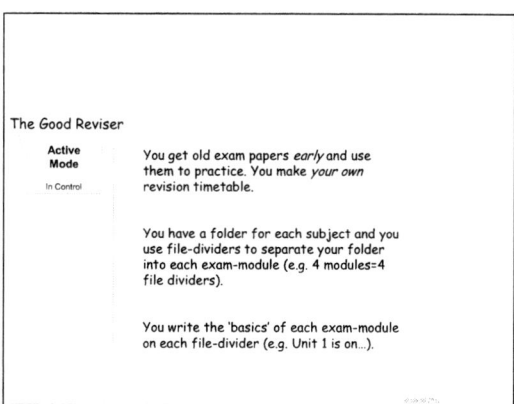

The 'Good Reviser' image (above) is an example of effective revision.

This helps students to clearly see what effective revision includes.

How do I use it...? Convert the image (above) to your own PowerPoint slide and display it on your whiteboard. Alternatively, enlarge the image, laminate it and display it in your room, ready for use.

When do I use it...? Use the 'Good Reviser' image when you are focusing on effective revision techniques.

**Revising**

plenary: self-reflection

Use the 'prompts' to talk about your active revising

" I find out what exam board I'm doing and go on their website so..."
" I focus on the subjects I need and the ones I struggle in which..."

Total Focus=overachievement

**Active Mode**

In Control

Use the 'prompts' to talk about your active-passive revising

" I do a revision timetable with help. It would be better if I..."
" I don't think about 'how long...?" or "which subjects...?" so I..."

Semi-focus=mixed achievement

**Active-Passive Mode**

Limited Control

Use the 'prompts' to talk about your passive revising

" I don't use revision timetables. I do 'last minute' revision but I..."
" I put revision off because I don't deal with stress well. This only..."

Unfocused=underachievement

**Passive Mode**

No Control

The 'Revising' plenary image (above) is a powerful way of students evaluating their current level of revision.

The plenary image also helps students to build a 'language of revision'.

If you look at the image (above), you'll notice that the sentences inside the boxes are incomplete.

The idea is that students decide where they are then complete the sentence to articulate their current level of revision.

The benefit of the plenary slide is that students need to communicate their understanding and, therefore, are beginning to become more aware of the importance of effective revision to success in school.

How do I use it...? Convert the image (above) to your own PowerPoint slide and display it on your whiteboard. Alternatively, enlarge the image, laminate it and display it in your room, ready for use.

When do I use it...? Use the 'Revising: plenary' image to help students link effective revision to successful learning.

Performing

in exams

A lot of people find performing in exams hard.

Performing can be made easier and less stressful if the skill of *visualising* your exam is used.

To find out more about *visualising* your exams, click on Performing 'Tips'.

The explanation image (above) on 'Performing' is designed for 'big picture' learners.

'Big picture' learners are concrete thinkers who need to able to visualise an idea in a practical situation.

The explanation for 'Performing' (above) paints a picture of what performing 'looks like' in school.

How do I use it…? Convert the image (above) to your own PowerPoint slide and display it on your whiteboard. Alternatively, enlarge the image, laminate it and display it in your room, ready for use.

When do I use it…? Think about using the explanation image as your starter when you are focusing on the importance of a performance mindset.

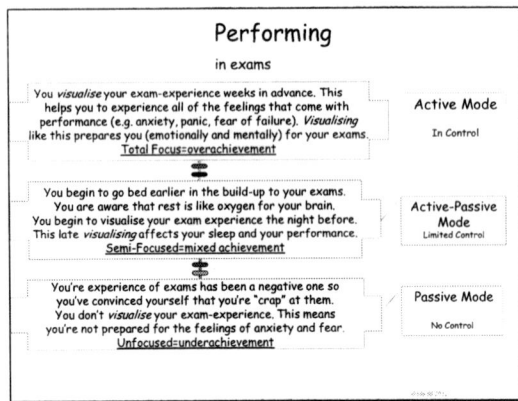

The '3 modes' image on 'Performing' (above) is like holding up a mirror for your students and helping them to reflect on their current level of performance in exams.

The small coloured boxes on the right-hand side highlight whether a student is in active, active-passive or passive mode. The use of these three modes helps students to see the impact of their current level of performance in exams.

How do I use it...? Convert the image (above) to your own PowerPoint slide and display it on your whiteboard. Alternatively, enlarge the image, laminate it and display it in your room, ready for use.

When do I use it...? Use the '3 modes' image when you are having a specific focus on developing a performance mindset.

**Performing 'Tips'**
for exams

The skill of *visualising*

1. imagine the night before your exams
   Why...? This will create the
   *performance feeling of anxiety.*

2. picture lining up outside the exam-hall
   Why...? This will create the
   performance *feeling of fear-of-failure.*

3. *Visualising* like this helps to prepare you
   emotionally and mentally for the *real
   thing*=success!

The 'Performing 'Tips'' image (above) is an example of an effective performance mindset.

This helps students to clearly see what effective performance includes.

How do I use it...? Convert the image (above) to your own PowerPoint slide and display it on your whiteboard. Alternatively, enlarge the image, laminate it and display it in your room, ready for use.

When do I use it...? Use the 'Performing 'Tips'' image when you are focusing on effective exam techniques.

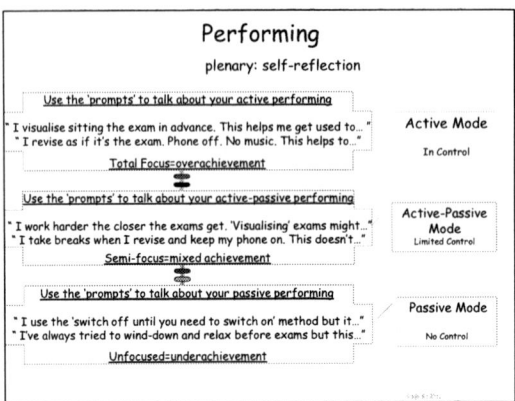

The 'Performing' plenary image (above) is a powerful way of students evaluating their current level of exam-performance.

The plenary image also helps students to build a 'language of performance'.

If you look at the image (above), you'll notice that the sentences inside the boxes are incomplete.

The idea is that students decide where they are then complete the sentence to articulate their current level of exam-performance.

The benefit of the plenary slide is that students need to communicate their understanding and, therefore, are beginning to become more aware of the importance of an effective performance-mindset to success in school.

How do I use it...? Convert the image (above) to your own PowerPoint slide and display it on your whiteboard. Alternatively, enlarge the image, laminate it and display it in your room, ready for use.

When do I use it...? Use the 'Performing: plenary' image to help students link an effective performance-mindset to successful learning.

Element 5 - Thinking

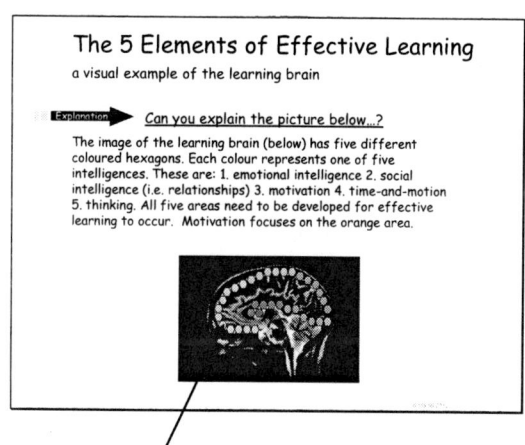

'Thinking' is the fifth of the five elements. In the image above, thinking is represented by the fifth section in the learning brain. There are six hexagons because each area has six skills. The six skills for 'Thinking' are:

1.Association   2.Interrogation   3.Hypothesis   4.Categorisation   5.Visualising   6.Hierarchy

Why is 'Thinking' element five...?

Because this is the final stage in the learning process. At this stage, students will have learnt to understand and manage their feelings (i.e. element one – emotional intelligence). They will have developed positive relationships with their teachers (i.e. element two – relationship skills). They will be internally motivated (i.e. element three – motivation). They will operate effectively in the classroom (i.e. element four – time-and-motion). With the first four elements in place, students will be ideally prepared to problem-solve. This is why it's the fifth element.

The fifth section of the book is, therefore, on the six thinking skills.

You will see an image above each page, providing with a resource to go along with the skill.

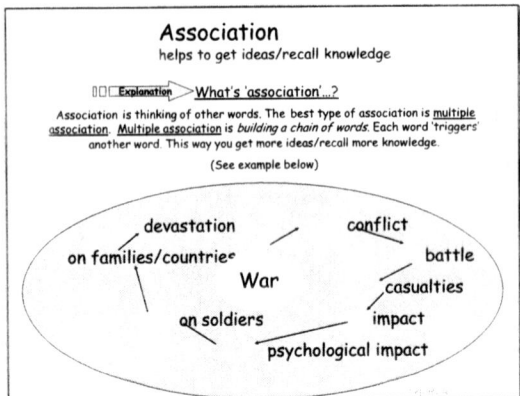

The explanation image (above) on 'Association' is designed for 'big picture' learners.

'Big picture' learners are concrete thinkers who need to able to visualise an idea in a practical situation.

The explanation for 'Association' (above) paints a picture of what association 'looks like' in school.

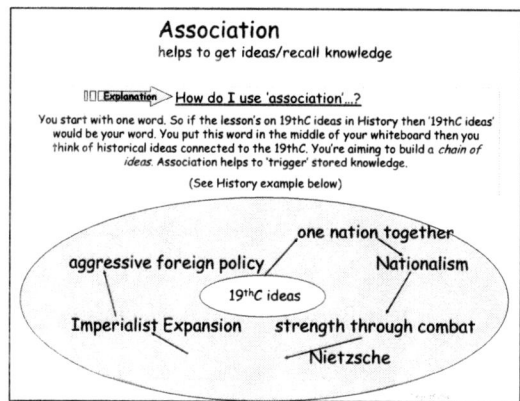

## How do use 'association' in lessons...?

The text-box in the image (above) helps with this: "You start with one word. So if the lesson's on 19thc ideas in History then '19<sup>th</sup>c ideas' would be the word your put in the middle of your whiteboard/PowerPoint slide. The aim is to build of chain of words (see example above). This chain of words will help students to re-call 'stored knowledge'.

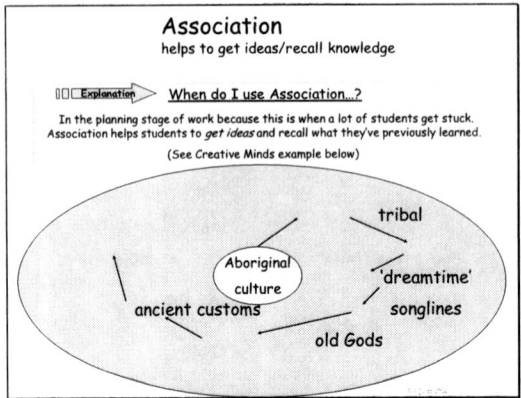

## When do I use 'association' in lessons..?

The text-box in the image (above) helps with this: "Use association in the planning stage because this is when a lot of students get stuck. Association helps students to generate ideas and recall 'stored knowledge.'"

**Association**
plenary: reflection

Use the 'prompts' to talk about your independent use of association

"In the planning stage, I associated to recall what I already knew so..."
"When I got stuck, instead of asking for help, I associated which..."
You overcome *all* barriers

Independent
Mode

Use the 'prompts' to talk about your inter-dependent use of association

"When got stuck, I needed to be reminded to associate so I next time..."
"I kept going back to the root word instead of branching off so I..."
You overcome *some* barriers

Inter-
dependent
Mode

Use the 'prompts' to talk about your dependent use of association

"I needed a visual example to start me off so next time I need to..."
"I asked for help as soon as I got stuck instead of associating ... next time."
You overcome no barriers

Dependent
Mode

The 'Association' plenary image (above) is a powerful way of students evaluating their current level of association.

The plenary image also helps students to build a 'language of association'.

If you look at the image (above), you'll notice that the sentences inside the boxes are incomplete.

The idea is that students decide where they are then complete the sentence to articulate their current level of association.

The benefit of the plenary slide is that students need to communicate their understanding and, therefore, are beginning to become more aware of the importance of association to independent learning.

How do I use it...? Convert the image (above) to your own PowerPoint slide and display it on your whiteboard. Alternatively, enlarge the image, laminate it and display it in your room, ready for use.

When do I use it...? Use the 'Association: plenary' image to help students make the link between association and creative thinking.

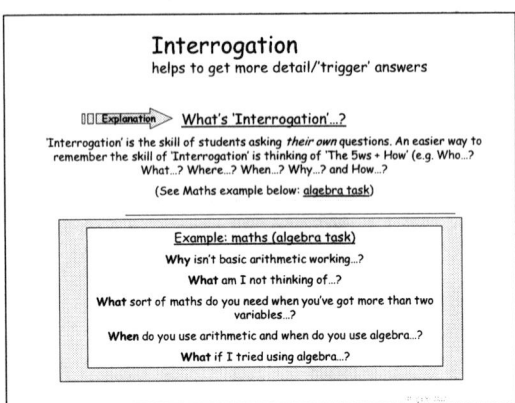

The explanation image (above) on 'Interrogation' is designed for 'big picture' learners.

'Big picture' learners are concrete thinkers who need to able to visualise an idea in a practical situation.

The explanation for 'Interrogation' (above) paints a picture of what interrogation 'looks like' in school.

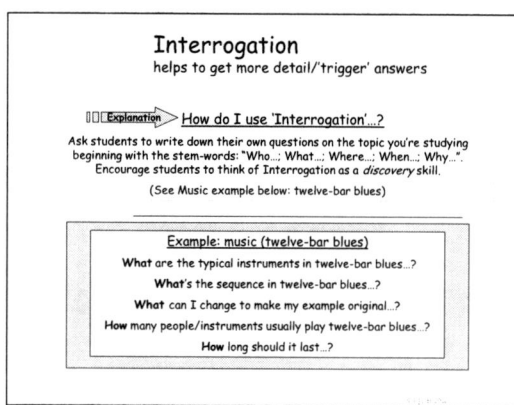

How do use 'interrogation' in lessons...?

The text-box in the image (above) helps with this: "Ask students to write down their own questions beginning with the stems: Who? What? Where? When? Why? How? Remind students that they are writing *their own questions*. Encourage students to think of interrogation as a 'discovery skill'.

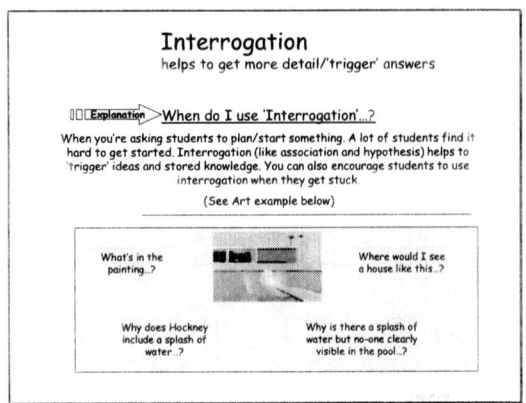

## When do I use 'association' in lessons..?

The text-box in the image (above) helps with this: "Use interrogation when you're asking students to plan/start something. A lot of students find it hard to get started. Interrogation (like association and hypothesis) helps to 'trigger ideas' and recall 'stored knowledge'. You can also encourage students to use interrogation when they get stuck – like a 'get-out-jail' thinking skill."

**Interrogation**
plenary: reflection

Use the 'prompts' to talk about your independent use of interrogation

"In the planning stage, I used interrogation to recall 'stored' knowledge so ..."
"When I got stuck, I used interrogation ... this helped me to..."

Independent Mode

You overcome *all* barriers

Use the 'prompts' to talk about your inter-dependent use of interrogation

"When I got stuck, I needed to be reminded to interrogate so next time I..."
"I thought interrogation was being given the questions. Now I know it's..."

Inter-dependent Mode

You overcome *some* barriers

Use the 'prompts' to talk about your dependent use of interrogation

"I asked for help as soon as I got stuck.. Next I need to use..."
"I always struggle to plan my work ... Now I know I can use..."

Dependent Mode

You overcome no barriers

The 'Interrogation' plenary image (above) is a powerful way of students evaluating their current level of interrogation.

The plenary image also helps students to build a 'language of interrogation'.

If you look at the image (above), you'll notice that the sentences inside the boxes are incomplete.

The idea is that students decide where they are then complete the sentence to articulate their current level of interrogation.

The benefit of the plenary slide is that students need to communicate their understanding and, therefore, are beginning to become more aware of the importance of interrogation to problem-solving and independent learning.

How do I use it...? Convert the image (above) to your own PowerPoint slide and display it on your whiteboard. Alternatively, enlarge the image, laminate it and display it in your room, ready for use.

When do I use it...? Use the 'Interrogation: plenary' image to help students make the link between interrogation and problem-solving.

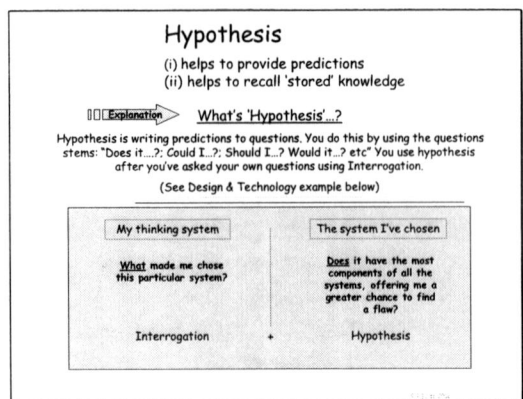

The explanation image (above) on 'Hypothesis' is designed for 'big picture' learners.

'Big picture' learners are concrete thinkers who need to able to visualise an idea in a practical situation.

The explanation for 'Hypothesis' (above) paints a picture of what hypothesis 'looks like' in school.

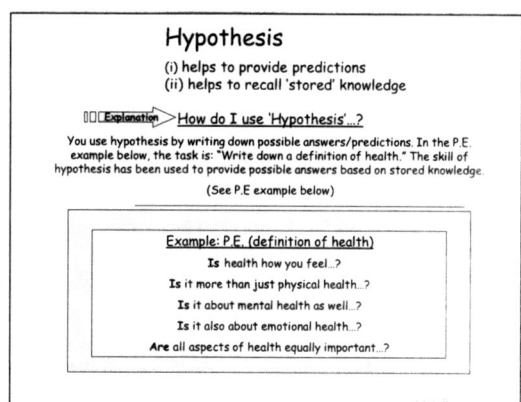

## How do use 'hypothesis' in lessons...?

The text-box in the image (above) helps with this: "You can use hypothesis by asking students to write possible answers/predictions to questions. In the P.E. example (above), the task is: 'Write down a definition of health'. The skill of hypothesis has been used to provide possible answers/predictions based on stored knowledge. It can be helpful to remind students that hypothesis is both a 'discovery and recovery' skill: i.e. it generates new ideas and recalls 'stored knowledge'.

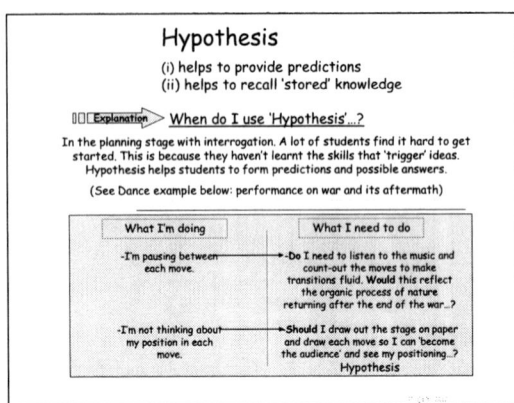

## When do I use 'hypothesis' in lessons..?

The text-box in the image (above) helps with this: "Use hypothesis in the planning stage along with interrogation. A lot of students find it hard to get started when faced with a new task. This is because they haven't learnt the skills which 'trigger ideas'. Hypothesis helps students to form predictions and possible answers." (see example above on Dance).

The 'Hypothesis' plenary image (above) is a powerful way of students evaluating their current level of hypothesis.

The plenary image also helps students to build a 'language of hypothesis'.

If you look at the image (above), you'll notice that the sentences inside the boxes are incomplete.

The idea is that students decide where they are then complete the sentence to articulate their current level of hypothesis.

The benefit of the plenary slide is that students need to communicate their understanding and, therefore, are beginning to become more aware of the importance of hypothesis to problem-solving.

How do I use it...? Convert the image (above) to your own PowerPoint slide and display it on your whiteboard. Alternatively, enlarge the image, laminate it and display it in your room, ready for use.

When do I use it...? Use the 'Hypothesis: plenary' image to help students make the link between hypothesis and analysis.

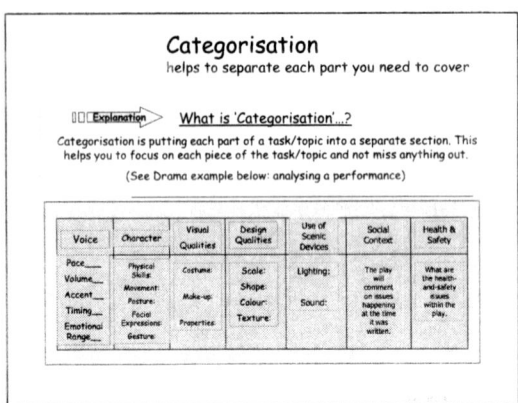

The explanation image (above) on 'Categorisation' is designed for 'big picture' learners.

'Big picture' learners are concrete thinkers who need to able to visualise an idea in a practical situation.

The explanation for 'Categorisation' (above) paints a picture of what categorisation 'looks like' in school.

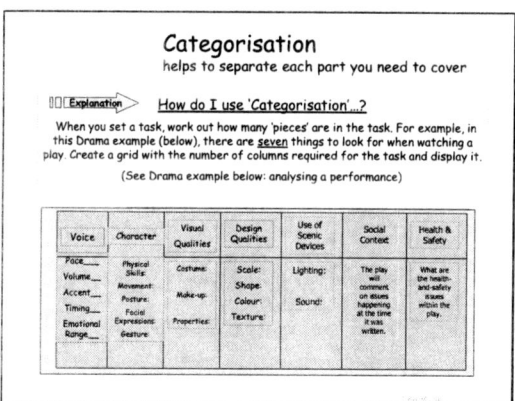

How do use 'categorisation' in lessons...?

The text-box in the image (above) helps with this: "When you set a task, work-out how many 'parts/pieces' you want students to focus on. For example, in the Drama example (above), there are <u>seven</u> things to look for when analysing a performance. Instead of bullet points, create a grid for the task: i.e. categorise each element into a column. Categorising tasks like this helps to structure students' thinking."

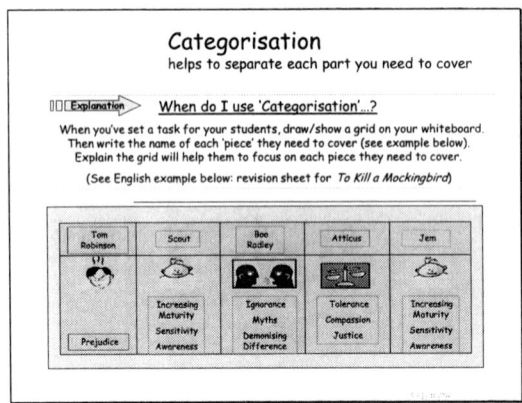

When do I use 'categorisation' in lessons..?

The text-box in the image (above) helps with this: "When you've set a task for your students, create a grid on your whiteboard/PowerPoint. Next, write the name of each part of the task you want students to focus on (see example above on *To Kill a Mockingbird*). Explain to students that categorising like this will help students to focus on each element and quickly see which ones they are covering/need to cover."

**Categorisation**
plenary: reflection

Use the 'prompts' to talk about your independent use of categorisation

"When I'm set something to do, I use categorisation to..."
"Categorisation helps me to 'block-out' key details. This is good because..."

You overcome *all* barriers

Independent Mode

Use the 'prompts' to talk about your inter-dependent use of categorisation

"I needed to ask how to set-out my work ... Next time I'll use ... because..."
"I used categorisation but I didn't know I was using it. It helps to know so..."

You overcome *some* barriers

Inter-dependent Mode

Use the 'prompts' to talk about your dependent use of categorisation

"I get confused and worked-up if I don't know how to start... Next time I'll..."
"I'm pretty organised and I think categorisation can help me because..."

You overcome no barriers

Dependent Mode

The 'Categorisation' plenary image (above) is a powerful way of students evaluating their current level of categorisation.

The plenary image also helps students to build a 'language of categorisation'.

If you look at the image (above), you'll notice that the sentences inside the boxes are incomplete.

The idea is that students decide where they are then complete the sentence to articulate their current level of categorisation.

The benefit of the plenary slide is that students need to communicate their understanding and, therefore, are beginning to become more aware of the importance of categorisation to organising ideas and information.

How do I use it...? Convert the image (above) to your own PowerPoint slide and display it on your whiteboard. Alternatively, enlarge the image, laminate it and display it in your room, ready for use.

When do I use it...? Use the 'Categorisation: plenary' image to help students make the link between categorisation and organising ideas and information.

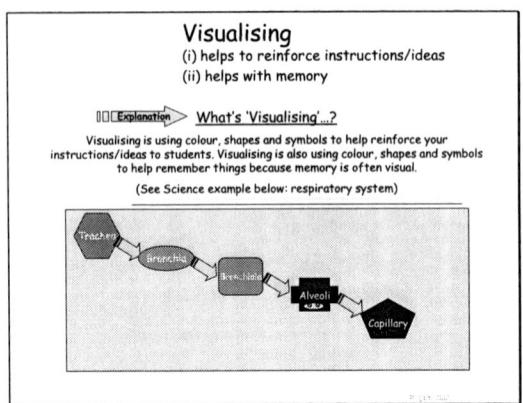

The explanation image (above) on 'Visualising' is designed for 'big picture' learners.

'Big picture' learners are concrete thinkers who need to able to visualise an idea in a practical situation.

The explanation for 'Visualising' (above) paints a picture of what visualising 'looks like' in school.

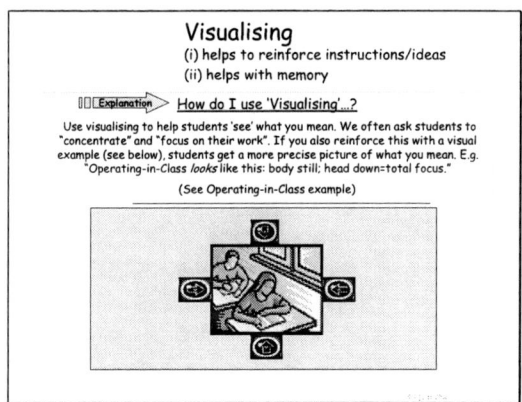

How do use 'visualising' in lessons...?

The text-box in the image (above) helps with this: "Use visualising to help students 'see' what you mean. We often ask students to 'concentrate' or 'focus on their work. If you reinforce this with a visual example (above), students get a more precise 'picture' of what you mean. Visualising is a key aspect of 'modelling': i.e. showing people what you mean. Modelling is a central aspect of learning. Many problems come from tasks not being modelled properly for students. Whenever you are introducing a new task, provide a visual model of what it 'looks like'."

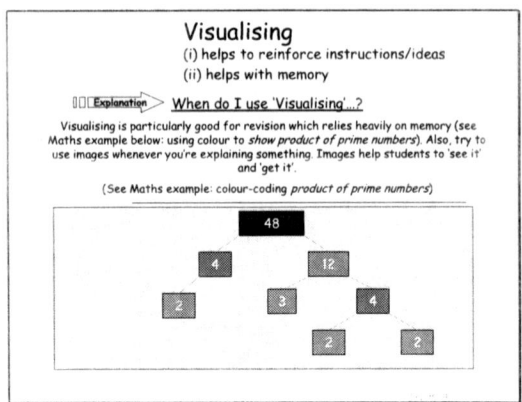

## When do I use 'visualising' in lessons..?

The text-box in the image (above) helps with this: "Visualising is particularly good for revision which relies heavily on memory. Also, try to use images whenever you're explaining something. Images help students to 'see it' and 'get it'. Visually modelling each task makes learning much easier for students."

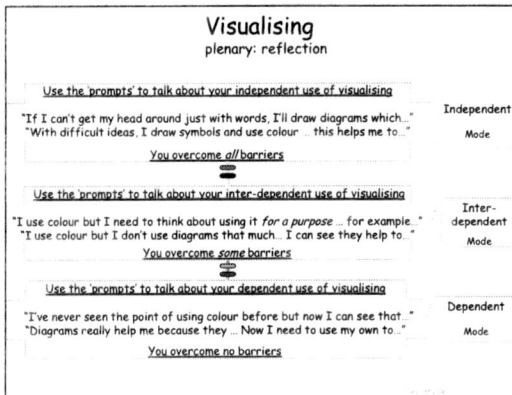

The 'Visualising' plenary image (above) is a powerful way of students evaluating their current level of visualising.

The plenary image also helps students to build a 'language of visualising'.

If you look at the image (above), you'll notice that the sentences inside the boxes are incomplete.

The idea is that students decide where they are then complete the sentence to articulate their current level of visualising.

The benefit of the plenary slide is that students need to communicate their understanding and, therefore, are beginning to become more aware of the importance of visualising to revision and memory-retention.

How do I use it...? Convert the image (above) to your own PowerPoint slide and display it on your whiteboard. Alternatively, enlarge the image, laminate it and display it in your room, ready for use.

When do I use it...? Use the 'Visualising: plenary' image to help students make the link between visualising and memory-retention

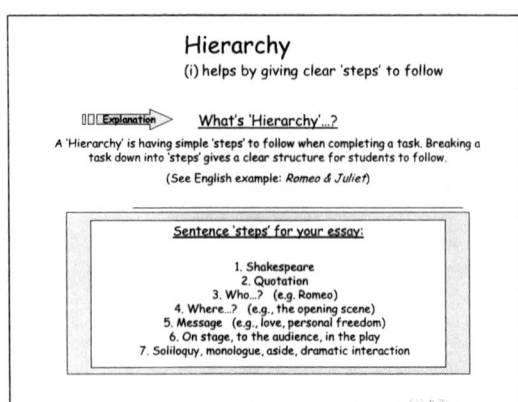

The explanation image (above) on 'Hierarchy' is designed for 'big picture' learners.

'Big picture' learners are concrete thinkers who need to able to visualise an idea in a practical situation.

The explanation for 'Hierarchy' (above) paints a picture of what hierarchy 'looks like' in school.

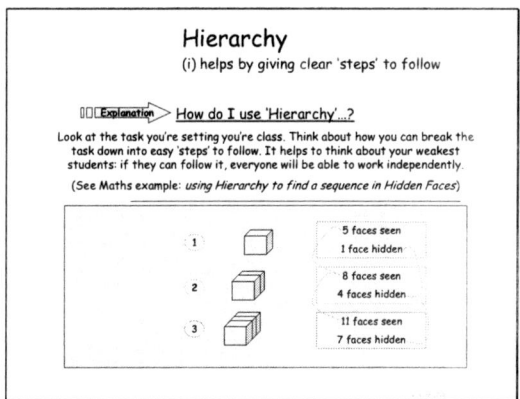

## How do use 'hierarchy' in lessons...?

The text-box in the image (above) helps with this: "Look at the task you're setting your class. Think about how you can break the task down into 'steps' to follow. It helps to think about your weakest students: i.e. if your weakest students can follow the 'steps' everyone will be able to understand them and work independently."

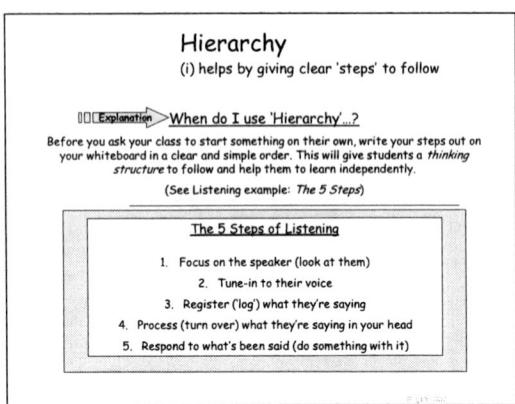

## When do I use 'hierarchy' in lessons..?

The text-box in the image (above) helps with this: "Before you ask your class to start something on their own, write your steps out on your whiteboard in a clear, simple order. This will give students a *thinking ladder* to follow which will help them to be more confident, independent learners."

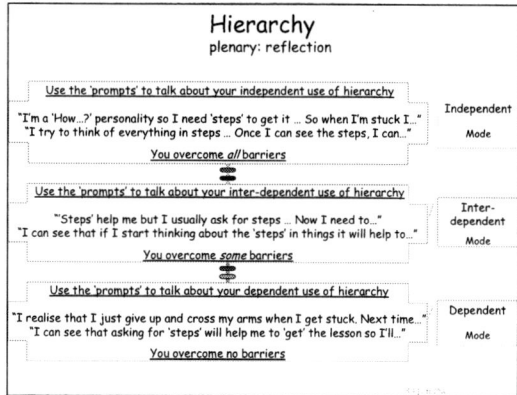

The 'Hierarchy' plenary image (above) is a powerful way of students evaluating their current level of hierarchy.

The plenary image also helps students to build a 'language of hierarchy'.

If you look at the image (above), you'll notice that the sentences inside the boxes are incomplete.

The idea is that students decide where they are then complete the sentence to articulate their current level of hierarchy.

The benefit of the plenary slide is that students need to communicate their understanding and, therefore, are beginning to become more aware of the importance of hierarchy to finding sequences (i.e. steps) in learning.

How do I use it...? Convert the image (above) to your own PowerPoint slide and display it on your whiteboard. Alternatively, enlarge the image, laminate it and display it in your room, ready for use.

When do I use it...? Use the 'Hierarchy: plenary' image to help students make the link between hierarchy and putting tasks into 'steps' to make learning easier.

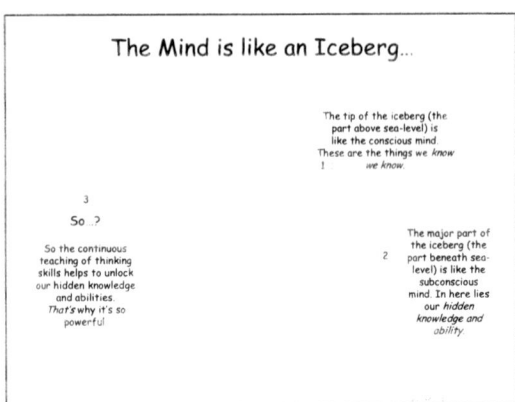

'The Mind is like an Iceberg' image (above) is a visual representation of the power of the subconscious mind in learning. The line at the top of the iceberg represents our conscious mind (visually from our neck upwards). Everything below the line represents our subconscious mind (visually from our neck downwards).

The power of the image is to show students how much of their learning is stored – not lost. Thinking skills such as: association, interrogation etc. Can 'trigger' this stored knowledge. Sometimes the knowledge is in our knees, sometimes deeper down in our ankles. However, by continuously using thinking skills, we can recall much a wealth of stored knowledge which makes us much better learners!

Conclusion

The aim of this book was to provide a deeper understanding of the way we learn – teachers and students.

The images on each page are designed to be copied and used. They have been used as:

1. Laminated cards for students as learning techniques
2. Included in teachers' PowerPoints to reinforce a particular skill in lessons
3. Laminated A3 posters displayed in classroom to reinforce certain focus skills
4. Laminated A3 posters displayed in school corridors to create a learning culture
5. Handbooks for parents to help them support their students at home
6. Handbooks for teachers in training-days to develop teachers' skill-base

I hope you've found the book useful and wish you every success in your teaching career.

Richard Lindo

March 2012

CPSIA information can be obtained at www.ICGtesting.com
Printed in the USA
LVOW10s1105140914

403987LV00002B/466/P